In Flora's Footsteps

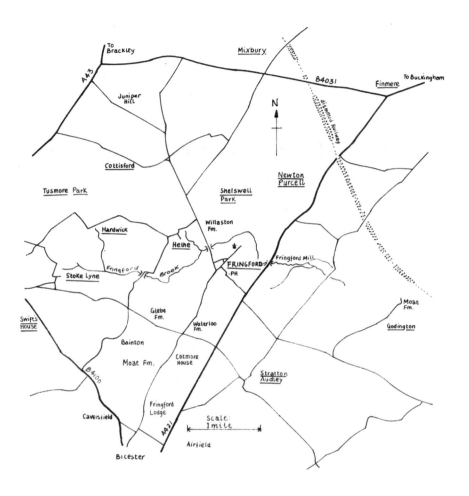

Lark Rise Country with the ten Shelswell parishes and three 'Great Houses' underlined.

In Flora's Footsteps

Daily Life in Lark Rise Country
1876–2009

Martin Greenwood

THE WYCHWOOD PRESS

Our books may be ordered from bookshops or (post free) from
The Wychwood Press, Alder House, Market Street, Charlbury, OX7 3PH
01608 811969

e-mail: wychwood@joncarpenter.co.uk

To order by credit card, please phone 01689 870437 or 01608 819117

www.wychwoodpress.co.uk

First published in 2009 by
The Wychwood Press
an imprint of Jon Carpenter Publishing
Alder House, Market Street, Charlbury, Oxfordshire OX7 3PH

Reprinted 2011 with minor corrections

ISBN   978 1 902279 37 4

Printed in England by CPI Antony Rowe, Chippenham

Contents

List of tables and illustrations   6

Foreword and acknowledgements   9

1 Lark Rise to Candleford: The BBC Television Series   13

2 Church and Chapel   23

3 The 'Great Houses'   36

4 'The Chase and the Turf'   51

5 Schools and Education   64

6 Changes in Village Life   74

7 The War Dead   95

8 Conclusion   105

Bibliography   108

Index   110

Tables

1. Religious Census 30 March 1851, Shelswell Parishes.   27
2. 2006 Church Attendance, Shelswell Parishes.   31
3. Shelswell Park: Domestic and Outdoor Staff 1851-1901.   38
4. Swift's House: Domestic and Outdoor Staff 1851-1901.   42
5. Tusmore Park: Domestic and Outdoor Staff 1851-1901.   46
6. Shelswell Schools 1824-2008.   66
7. Population in the Shelswell Group 1801-2001.   76
8. Shelswell Farms 1852-1939.   81

Illustrations

Flora Thompson c.1903.   8
The End House, Juniper Hill (Lark Rise), 1950s.   16
Queenie Massey, 1880.   17
Elizabeth Hinks, with her lace pillow and bobbins, late 1920s.   17
Cottisford House, 1981.   19
Fringford Post Office and Forge c.1890.   20
Frederick Plumb (Matthew) with Thomas Deeley c.1910.   21
Edward Slater-Harrison (Sir Timothy) in riding gear, 1903.   21
Cottisford (Fordlow) Church, 1979.   23
Fringford (Candleford Green) Church c.1920.   28
Fringford Ladies Cricket XI c.1915.   29
Hethe Methodist Chapel, early 1960s.   32
Hethe Roman Catholic Chapel, early 1960s.   34
Shelswell House, 1901.   37
Edward Slater-Harrison (Sir Timothy) with his coach & four, 1902.   39
Swift's House, Stoke Lyne, 1950s.   41
Tusmore Park, 1912.   44
Nurses at Tusmore Park during the Second World War.   45
War Service Award to Joan Coles (née Staniforth).   47
Mrs Margaret Lloyd-Mostyn in her pony and trap, 1940s.   56
Charlie Johnson and Mrs Margaret Lloyd-Mostyn, early 1950s.   56
The Old Forge, Fringford c.1898.   57
Col. George Gosling, 1914.   59
GWR advertisement for the Hunting Season, 1903.   61
Cottisford School, 1905.   65
Fringford May Queen, early 1950s.   67
Fringford Old School, 1920s.   68
Schoolchildren in front of Fringford school c.1910.   69
Certificate given to Mrs Emily Hinks for providing a home to evacuees. 70

Stratton Audley School, 1905.   72
The Wyatt family, Manor Farm, Hethe c.1910.   77
Thomas Hanks Allen threshing at Waterloo Farm, 1920s.   78
Fringford Mill, sheep washing, 1920s.   79
Fringford Mill, cleaning party, c.1920.   80
Mrs Omar's shop, Fringford, 1950s.   84
Hethe Post Office and Shop, early 1960s.   84
T.H. Allen cycle, radio and repair shop, Hethe, early 1960s.   85
Reuben Judd and his sons, Newton Purcell, early 1900s.   88
The Oddfellows' procession leaving Fringford church c.1900-10.   91
Card printed on the death of Edwin (Edmund) Timms, 26 April 1916.   104

Colour photographs and illustrations (after page 64)

Laura (Olivia Hallinan) in the BBC television series, 2008.   (i)
Twister (Karl Johnson) and Queenie (Linda Bassett) in the BBC television
    series, 2008.   (ii)
Dorcas Lane (Julia Sawalha) and Sir Timothy (Ben Miles) in the BBC televi-
    sion series, 2008.   (iii)
The cast-iron cross marking the grave of Zilpha Hinks (Zillah), 1900.   (iv)
Fringford Old Rectory.   (v)
Collage of the ten Shelswell Churches, 2008.   (vi)-(vii)
Shelswell Park stable block after its restoration in 2000.   (viii)
Tusmore Park, 2005.   (ix)
J. & C. Walker's Fox Hunting Map of Buckinghamshire, 1830s.   (x)
Fringford Old School, 2007.   (xi)
Newton Purcell School, 1971.   (xi)
Thatched cottages, Main Street, Fringford, 2007.   (xii)
Old Bake House, Fringford, 2007.   (xii)
Dew's Store, Fritwell, said to have been the largest village store in England.   (xiii)
Banner of the Mansfield Lodge of the Independent Order of the Oddfellows
    (Manchester Unity).   (xiv)-(xv)
'Motor House 1902', Tusmore Park.   (xvi)

Flora Thompson, possibly c. 1903 when she married John Thompson. (Violet McGovern)

Foreword and
Acknowledgements

'She was never to see any of these [landmarks] again, but she was
to carry a mental picture of them, to be recalled at will, through
the changing scenes of a lifetime.'[1]

Flora Thompson wrote this on the final page of *Lark Rise to Candleford*,
as she remembered her last visit to Lark Rise (Juniper Hill), where she
had been born in 1876. The recent BBC television series has now brought
her unique recollections of rural life in the late nineteenth century to the
attention of millions. Many of them no doubt were already fans, or at least
familiar with her work, but there must be thousands of new ones. The
series has raised some confusion in people's minds about the relationship
between it and Flora's original book. Some of the characters' names have
been changed and the forge has been placed in the town of Candleford,
not the village of Candleford Green. As a resident of Fringford and a local
historian for nearly twenty years, I have been fortunate to become very
familiar with the three villages associated with Flora's early life, Juniper
Hill (Lark Rise), Cottisford (Fordlow) and Fringford (Candleford Green).
This has encouraged me to compare the BBC series with the original book
and look at it in relation to the history of these villages. At the same time,
it has provided a perfect starting point to take a wider look at daily life in
Lark Rise and its surrounding villages, what might be called 'Lark Rise
country' in hunting terms.

In Chaper 1, I examine the possible confusion between the series and
the original book. I also provide some guidance to those who may wish
to trace on the ground some of the events and places mentioned in the
series. In the following chapters, I look at daily life in Lark Rise country,
focusing on the major influences and changes during and after Flora's
Victorian childhood. As I explain in Chapter 2, Lark Rise and its
surrounding villages are now part of the Shelswell Group (now the
Shelswell Benefice) of parishes. I examine the formation of this group,

which provides a new unity for ten villages, at least for religious purposes. It is clear, however, that there were many links between these parishes in the nineteenth century and probably much earlier. I examine the history of the churches and chapels in these parishes, including the presence of the Methodists and Roman Catholics. I look at the changes arising from the new benefice structure, and the problems of declining attendance. I also look at what the future might hold for our local parishes.

In Chapter 3, I look at the influence of three 'Great Houses' in the area: Shelswell Park, Swift's House and Tusmore Park. Strictly speaking, none of these has ever been a Great House, like Blenheim or Stowe, but they would have seemed so to the local inhabitants. They have been large enough to have their own supporting communities, while also being dependent on the surrounding villages for a variety of services. In Chapter 4, I look at the history of the Bicester Hunt, which has had close links with these and other large houses in the area, and has had a significant influence on local community life for well over two hundred years. Over this period, the Hunt's kennels have been variously located in Bainton, Swift's House, and now in Stratton Audley, all within the Shelswell Group. The Hunt has always provided employment for local people and continues to do so, in spite of the recent anti-hunting legislation. I also look at some of the local connections with 'the Turf'.

In Chapter 5, I look at the history of schools and education in the Group, including the various reorganisations and the steady decline in the number of schools, so that there are now only two primary schools. I also examine the effect of the influx of evacuees during the Second World War. In Chapter 6, I take a wider look at some of the changes in village life since the mid-nineteenth century, including the decline in rural populations and changes in work and employment. I examine the major part played by agriculture in providing both direct employment and support for a number of related trades. I look at the number and names of the local farms and how life has changed for them. Finally, in Chapter 7, I look at the names and personal details of the War Dead for all the ten parishes, as far as they are available. I hope that listing and examining these details may help to put into context just how devastating the losses in the two World Wars were for the local communities.

As a resident of Fringford, I have not presumed to try and write a history of the other nine parishes in the Group. Other people have done and are doing serious research on at least some of those villages, and I am grateful to them for access to their work. I only hope that readers may enjoy this broader examination of daily life in Lark Rise and its surrounding villages. I have no doubt that Flora would be amazed at some of the changes and also at our interest in her work, which provides such a unique starting point for looking at village life.

I am extremely grateful to all those who have helped me in my research for this book.

I am particularly grateful to the following: Margaret Allen, Ted Flaxman, Gladys Hinks, Kathleen Hunt, Norah Morgan, David Taylor, Mary Morgan, Pauline O'Gorman, Violet McGovern, Jo Templer, Albert Parker, and Malcolm and Judith Harvey from the End House. I would like to thank the Baroness Ann von Maltzahn for information on the Shelswell estate and for use of her photographs. I am grateful to Becky Adams and the Revd Ricky Yates for their help on the Shelswell Benefice. I would like to thank Sheila Johnson for her memories of the Bicester Hunt and Joan Staniforth for her memories of the Tusmore Hospital. I am grateful to Jean Nicholls for allowing me access to the records of the Buckingham Oddfellows' Lodges. I must mention my debt to Tony Webster, as curator of the Flora Thompson Exhibition at the Old Gaol in Buckingham, for sharing his knowledge of Flora and her works. I would also like to acknowledge my debt to Christine Bloxham for her invaluable book, *The World of Flora Thompson Revisited*, and to Bill Gallagher, the writer and producer of the BBC television series, for his recent talk and support.

I would like to thank Malcolm Graham, Carl Boardman and the staff at Oxfordshire Studies for their patience and assistance in answering my queries and allowing me to use some photographs from the collections of the Oxfordshire County Council Photographic Archive (OCC). I would also like to thank the BBC Photo Library and the actors involved for permission to use some images from the first television series of *Lark Rise to Candleford*. I am very grateful to Wafic Said for allowing me to use a photograph of Tusmore Park in 1912, and to him and June Buck / *Country Life* for a photograph of the new Tusmore Park. I am grateful to the *Oxford Mail* and *Oxford Times* for a photograph of the End House. I must also thank Brenda Long for the old photograph of Swift's House. I am extremely grateful to the Greening Lamborn Trust for their generous grant towards the cost of reproducing all these photographs.

I am very grateful to Julie Barrett for the map and for her beautiful paintings, and to her and the other artists for the collage of the Shelswell churches. I must thank Mike Barrett for his excellent photographic skills and Peter Silver for his skilled assistance in scanning and assembling all the photographs for publication. I would like to thank James Nash for his rigorous reading of the text and his suggestions for improvement. I am hugely indebted to Jon Carpenter for agreeing to publish this book and for his help and encouragement along the way. Finally, I must thank my wife, Anne, for all her patience while I have been researching and writing this book.

Martin Greenwood
Fringford, March 2009

Notes

1   Flora Thompson, *Lark Rise to Candleford*, 537.

Chapter 1

Lark Rise to Candleford: The BBC TV Series

'Poverty's no disgrace, but 'tis a great inconvenience.'[1]

This short phrase somehow conveys perfectly the nature of life in Lark Rise. The hamlet had been created originally for the poor who were not wanted by the middle class of Cottisford and poverty was very much part of daily life. The phrase also illustrates the genius of Flora Thompson's writing, where such memorable phrases leap from every page. The BBC television series has brought Flora's unique picture of rural life in the late nineteenth century to the attention of millions.

Lark Rise to Candleford was originally published as three separate books: *Lark Rise* (1939), *Over to Candleford Green* (1941), and *Candleford Green* (1943), and published as a trilogy in 1945. In the books *Laura* (representing Flora herself) recalls her childhood in the hamlet of *Lark Rise* (Juniper Hill) and at school in *Fordlow* (Cottisford) before moving to *Candleford Green* (Fringford), where she worked in the village post office from 1891 to 1897. It is a vivid picture of village life at the end of the nineteenth century and, uniquely, it was written by 'a child of poverty', who was able to avoid any sense of bitterness against the squire and his class. Not only was it published by the Oxford University Press but it also received a magnificent testimonial from the publisher, Sir Humphrey Milord. He considered that the two most important books he had published in his twenty-two years at the Press were Arnold Toynbee's *A Study of History* and Flora Thompson's *Lark Rise to Candleford*.

As Bill Gallagher, the writer and producer of the series, explained in a recent talk to a local audience, it has taken some ten years to bring Lark Rise to our screens. He has a passion for the book, which shows in the skill of the adaptation and the superb performances by many of the cast. As he would agree, open any page and a wonderful character and story leap from it. This makes the book ideal for a series of episodes rather than a narrative approach. However, some confusion has arisen about the relationship between the series and the original book, although the BBC has made it clear that the series is 'based on' the book. Some of the key names have been changed and the series starts with Laura's move to Candleford rather than her childhood in Lark Rise. Crucially, the Old Forge and Post Office, where Flora worked, has been placed in the town of Candleford rather than the village of Candleford Green (Fringford). Candleford is always seen as an amalgam of Bicester, Buckingham and Brackley.

Gallagher has explained the thinking behind this decision. He saw Laura's move as a dramatic point when she enters the new world and new values of Candleford and leaves behind the old world and old values of Lark Rise. This change is emphasised by placing the Old Forge in the town of Candleford rather than the village of Candleford Green. Flora wrote of her move as follows: 'In the hamlet there lived only one class of people; all did similar work, all were poor and all equal. The population of Candleford Green was more varied.'[2] There has been some dismay locally that the series has been filmed in Wiltshire and Gloucestershire rather than Oxfordshire. However, as Gallagher has explained, permanent sets have been built for Lark Rise and Candleford. This means that these can be used at any time without interruption, which there would be if local dwellings and settings were used. Given the number of series planned, this will be of great benefit to the production team.

Given some of the misconceptions about the series, it seems sensible to look at the reality of village life in the period when Flora was growing up. In many respects, village life had changed very little in the decades before 1876 when Flora was born. Deference to those above you was the norm and 'Every member of the community knew his or her place and few wished to change it.'[3] It was a defining moment just before the agricultural depressions of the 1870s and 1890s and before the impact of major changes in health, housing and education.

It is generally accepted that the original book is largely autobiographical and a very accurate picture of Flora's childhood, particularly in the early chapters about Juniper Hill (Lark Rise) and Cottisford (Fordlow). Her early years here have not been covered so far by the BBC series, although Lark Rise does play a significant part in most of the instalments. Overall, the portrayal of Lark Rise does raise some questions, although these are not necessarily criticisms. The country scenes are in some ways too idyllic and 'chocolate box', although there are signs of the real poverty experienced by most of the inhabitants. Sue Braby goes to the workhouse, when her husband is sent to prison, there is an evident lack of food, and there is some indication of the large number of children in most of the small cottages. In the following paragraphs, I look briefly at the history of the three communities, and compare the portrayals by Flora and the BBC.

Juniper Hill (Lark Rise)

It is worth recalling briefly the humble origins of Juniper Hill, which has always been part of the parish of Cottisford. In 1754, two cottages were built on 'the Rise', part of the former Cottisford Heath, for the poor. Two more were built soon afterwards, as Cottisford attempted to remove the poor from their village. After this 'The Hamlet' stagnated until the mid-nineteenth century. It was always a poor community, 'the spot God made with the left-overs when He'd finished creating the rest of the earth'[4] and a natural home for squatters. That said, the people were willing to enjoy life despite being poor, and seemed to have the 'the lost secret of being happy on a little'. Their lives were guided by the light of a few homely precepts, such as 'Pay your way and fear nobody', 'Honesty's the best policy' and 'Don't flinch'.[5] My grandmother, who was also born in the 1870s, was guided in much the same way.

In 1853 the hamlet suddenly became the focus of attention. There was furious opposition by the 'Juniper Hill Mob' to enclosure of the Common, culminating in the 'Cottisford Riots'. A letter of Flora's in 1930 indicates why this opposition may have been so violent. In it she refers to a widespread belief among the old people that the former Cottisford heath had been left to the poor, and the deeds hidden behind the brass in the village church, 'from whence it was stolen'. In any event, after a summer of discontent, during which warrants of ejection were issued against forty-two men, a compromise was reached. This allowed the cottagers to harvest the current year's crops and gave them a 14-year lease on their dwellings at a nominal rent of 5s. per annum. Also, four small freeholders with proof of ownership were allocated plots under the enclosure award.

Enclosure was finally completed in 1856. There were now 20 small owners of land or cottages, of whom 17 had been issued with ejection orders three years before. Most of them were members of the Moss, Savin and Tuffrey families. By Flora's time in 1881, there were 35 houses including an inn, with a population of 127. This was just over half the total of people living in the parish of Cottisford. Most of the houses had been built on land ceded as 'squatters' rights'. You might say that it had

The End House, Juniper Hill (Lark Rise), where Flora Thompson grew up, 1950s. (Oxford Mail & Oxford Times)

been a victory for the squatters, but there must have been an uneasy peace with the village of Cottisford.

'In the hamlet there lived only one class of people; all did similar work, all were poor and all equal.'[6] It should be said, however, that the Timms in the End House were not quite as poor or equal as the rest. Flora's father, Albert, worked as a stonemason and his wages put the family a cut above all the agricultural labourers. Flora was also soon to discover for herself that 'the population of Candleford Green was more varied' and life there 'as distinct from that of a hamlet as the life of a country town was from that of a city.'[7]

A century later, in 1999, some 35% of the parish of Cottisford were living here in 21 dwellings.[8] There has been a marked improvement and enlargement of the houses and many of the old cottages have been demolished. There is certainly no 'affordable housing', as the authorities are looking for today! In Flora's day the original houses were in a ring on the Common. Hence the people were used to 'going round the Rise'[9] and it is still possible to do this. Many of the allotments survive and the size and

Queenie Massey, the beewoman and lace-maker, in 1880. (Eva Bateman)

situation of the hamlet is not much changed. The Fox Inn ('The Waggon and Horses'), however, closed more than a decade ago and at the End House only one original wall remains, although there is a blue plaque to Flora. There are now few larks or juniper bushes, although a bush survives at the Old Fox, and a new one has been planted at the End House.

When we come to the Lark Rise characters in the series, it is fair to say that most of them do appear in the book, although many of the names have been changed. Albert Timms, Flora's father, becomes Robert Timmins but his character, as difficult and possibly alcoholic with outspoken Liberal views, is authentic. In some cases, like Dawn French's Sue Braby, the original character, Caroline Arless, makes only a fleeting appearance in the book. Some might wish that it had been more fleeting in the first series but she did bring something different and lively to the screen! Flora's Queenie and Twister Macey were based on Eliza and Thomas Massey, who lived on the lane in front of the End House, in a cottage which is still called Queenie's. In the series their surname has been changed to Turrill but their characters are very much the same as in the book. Queenie is beautifully recalled in the book 'tanging the bees' with her

Elizabeth Hinks, with her lace pillow and bobbins, like Queenie in Lark Rise. She is sitting with Willam 'Joe' Spacey in front of her cottage in Mansfield Yard, Fringford, late 1920s. (Gladys Hinks)

spoon on the coal shovel, while 'her lace-making was a constant attraction to the children. They loved to see the bobbins tossed hither and thither, at random as it seemed to them, every bobbin weighted with its bright bunch of beads and every bunch with its own story…'.[10] Sadly she died in the Bicester Workhouse in 1902, aged eighty-one.

I hope that this gives a flavour of the original Lark Rise and its inhabitants, and that it may help those who want to walk in Flora's footsteps. You can continue in her steps and walk across the fields to Cottisford (Fordlow), as she did with her brother, Edwin, when he first started school. She was worried that he might be bullied if they walked with the others on the road. In the event, he was well able to take care of himself, and later became a soldier. He died in Flanders, near Ypres, in 1916 — a tragedy for Flora, who was devoted to her brother.

Cottisford (Fordlow)

The village of Fordlow has hardly figured in the series, as we have not seen any portrayal of Flora's early childhood and attendance at Fordlow School. The old and very conservative rector, Charles Harrison (Mr Ellison) has made a brief appearance, while his daughter figures more often, as she marries the rather splendid Revivalist postman, Thomas Brown. An imaginary story but Thomas Brown does appear in the book, as a recent convert to Methodism and a local preacher.[11]

Cottisford village, like its rector, was very conservative, with little consideration for the poor, who, as we have seen, were banished to Lark Rise. There was also stern disapproval of any religious dissent, as we shall see in a later chapter. The attitude of the gentry is typified by the treatment of the area round the churchyard. Until the 1820s, the churchyard was enclosed by cottages on three sides. In about 1825 William Turner took the lease of Cottisford House, altered the roads and demolished the cottages to lay out pleasure gardens. The occupants of the cottages were re-housed in a group of cottages known as The Warren, which was situated on the north side of the village, about half a mile from the crossroads by the school. Today there is no trace of it. There was similar re-housing in places like Middleton Stoney and Nuneham Courtenay, where the owners wished to develop their parks and gardens. It is also worth mentioning 'the row of model cottages occupied by the shepherd, the blacksmith, and other superior farm-workers.'[12] These were built across from the school by the Earl of Effingham in 1870. They were certainly not for the poor or average farm worker.

Cottisford House, which Flora visited on the annual school treat, 1981. (OCC)

Today, the village is little changed and still dominated by the large houses: Cottisford House with its 'pleasure gardens', where the school children went to tea once a year, Manor and College Farms and the Old Rectory. The school, at the crossroads, was finally closed in 1968. Sadly, subsequent conversion to a private dwelling, with numerous alterations and extensions, has removed almost all the features of the old school building.

If you wish to walk from here to Fringford (Candleford Green), the scenic route takes you across Shelswell Park, the home of Edward Slater-Harrison (Sir Timothy) in Flora's day. Be warned, however, there are a great many stiles! If you drive, you will see the park on your left but the big house was abandoned in the 1960s and finally pulled down in the late 1970s. Only the fine stable block survives.

Fringford (Candleford Green)

As we have noted, the BBC series moves the Forge and Post Office, where Flora worked from 1891 to 1897, from the village of Candleford Green to the urban Candleford. So it may come as a surprise to some to find the Old Forge located in the rural setting of Fringford. Candleford is an amalgam of Bicester, Brackley and Buckingham, all of which Flora had visited. In contrast, much of Candleford Green is an authentic and vivid account of Fringford in the 1890s. You can still see the Old Forge, the Church, the

Fringford Post Office and Forge c.1890, with John and Kesia Whitton (Dorcas Lane) standing by the cart. Zilpha Hinks (Zillah) stands in the doorway; William Elderfield, the watchmender, is standing on the far left with a sledgehammer on his shoulder. Frederick Plumb (Matthew the Foreman)), is third from left. (Bill Plumb)

Manor, the Old Rectory, the Old School, and the old farmhouses grouped round the Green. However, you will not find 'Chestnut Avenue' with its chestnut trees and modern suburban villas, or the 'Miss Pratt's' drapery and fashion shop, both imported from suburbia into the book.

Flora's stories about 'Miss Lane's Forge and Post Office' all seem authentic. Kesia Whitton (Dorcas Lane), who ran it, may have been 18 stone (some 250 pounds) but in other respects Flora's portrayal was very accurate, as she herself confirmed. Kesia was the daughter of Alex Kirby, the Stoke Lyne blacksmith, and a powerful character by all accounts. 'Had she lived a century earlier or half a century later, she would probably have been found in the forge with a sledge-hammer in her hand for she had an indomitable energy and a passion for doing and making things.' "Clever" was the general village description of her. "She's a clever one, that Miss Lane, as sharp as vinegar, but not bad in her way," people would afterwards say to Laura. Only her two or three enemies said that if she had lived at one time she'd have been burned as a witch.'[13] She was clearly a great influence on the young Flora and encouraged her avid reading. 'Matthew the Foreman' (Frederick Plumb) and the other characters in the forge also ring true, as does the description of the forge itself. The old servant 'Zillah',

Frederick Plumb (Matthew) with Thomas Deeley (smock) in the garden of the Old Forge, c.1910. Note the privy in the background. (Bill Plumb)

however, was based on Zilpha Hinks, who was only 36 when Flora arrived at the Forge. She was to die in 1900 aged 45, shortly after Flora left. She is buried in Fringford churchyard, where her cast-iron cross is just inside the gate.

Flora's portrayal of Edward Slater-Harrison (Sir Timothy), at Shelswell Park, where Flora signed on as an employee of the Post Office, seems authentic: 'She sensed the atmosphere of jollity, good sense, and good nature, together with the smell of tobacco, stables, and country tweeds he carried around like an aura.'[14]
However, the romance between him and Dorcas Lane in the series is of course imaginary and highly unlikely, although it makes a very good story-line. Cecilia Slater-Harrison (Lady Adelaide), Edward's first wife, also makes a brief appearance in the book. She would occasionally come into the post office herself, rather than getting her footman to do the business. 'She would come rustling in, bringing with her a whiff of perfume, and sink languidly down in the chair provided for customers. She was a graceful woman and it was a delight to watch her movements. She was tall and thin and, Laura thought, aristocratic-

Edward Slater-Harrison (Sir Timothy) in riding gear, outside Shelswell House, 1903. (OCC)

looking.'[15] She was in her sixties by this time and there was certainly no question of her being desperate for a child, as shown in the series.

I hope that these comments may help to shed some light on the three communities and to correct some of the possible misconceptions arising from the television series. I hope too that it may encourage more people to walk in the steps of Flora and read her great book. In the following chapters, I look at some of the major changes in rural life in Lark Rise and its surrounding villages since Flora's Victorian childhood, and how there was a wider sense of community well before the formation of the Shelswell Group of parishes.

Notes

1   Flora Thompson, *Lark Rise to Candleford*, 31.
2   Thompson, *Lark Rise*, 416.
3   Thompson, *Lark Rise*, 417.
4   Thompson, *Lark Rise*, 254.
5   Thompson, *Lark Rise*, 219.
6   Thompson, *Lark Rise*, 416.
7   Thompson, *Lark Rise*, 416.
8   Ted & Joan Flaxman, *Cottisford Revisited*, 10.
9   Thompson, *Lark Rise*, 18.
10   Thompson, *Lark Rise*, 82-3.
11   Thompson, *Lark Rise*, 407-8.
12   Thompson, *Lark Rise*, 177.
13   Thompson, *Lark Rise*, 394-5.
14   Thompson, *Lark Rise*, 415.
15   Thompson, *Lark Rise*, 465.

Chapter 2

Church and Chapel

'The afternoon service, with not a prayer left out or a creed spared,
seemed to the children everlasting.'[1]

Flora and her brother Edwin had to sit through a regular sermon of forty-five minutes from the Revd Charles Harrison (Mr Ellison) in Cottisford (Fordlow). He was a parson of the old school, who 'was as far as possible removed by birth, education, and worldly circumstances from the lambs of his flock.'[2] One of his favourite subjects was the supreme rightness of the social order as it then existed. This was perfectly demonstrated by the seating of the congregation, which saw the squire and vicar's families seated in the chancel, while the rank and file sat in the nave 'nicely graded, with the farmer's family in the front row, then the Squire's gardener and coachman, the schoolmistress, the maidservants, and the cottagers, with the Parish Clerk at the back to keep order.'[3]

Once and once only did inspiration move him, after the polling for the General Election of 1886. He had begun one of his usual sermons on the duty to social superiors, when he was suddenly moved with righteous anger and 'roared, "There are some among you who have lately forgotten that duty, and we know the cause, the *bloody cause!*" Laura shivered. Bad language in church! and from the Rector! But,

Cottisford (Fordlow) Church, where Flora once heard the Revd Charles Harrison (Mr Ellison) use bad language, 1979. (OCC)

later in life, she liked to think that she had lived early enough to have heard a mild and orthodox Liberalism denounced from the pulpit as "a bloody cause". It lent her the dignity of an historical survival.'[4] The Church of England may have hoped that most people were attending at least some of these services. The reality was very different, as we shall see in examining the results of the Religious Census of 1851. Before we do this, it is time to explain the origins of the Shelswell Group of parishes.

The Group Ministry

In 1983 the Shelswell Group Ministry was formally established for religious purposes. At that stage it was divided into the North Benefice (Cottisford, Finmere with Mixbury, Hardwick-with-Tusmore, and Newton Purcell-with-Shelswell) and the South Benefice (Fringford, Godington, Hethe, Stoke Lyne and Stratton Audley). In 1995 the Benefice of Shelswell was created, with ten parishes under one rector, the Revd Warwick (Ricky) Yates. It has to be said that the term 'benefice', which means strictly a 'church living', is a somewhat strange title to denote a group of parishes. In France, as I understand it, the term 'super parish' is used and this might have been more intelligible.

In 2001 there were two formal mergers, between the parishes of Godington and Stratton Audley, and the parishes of Cottisford and Hardwick-with-Tusmore. It is worth mentioning here that Flora would have known something about all these parishes and had particular links with a number of them. As we have seen, she grew up in Juniper Hill, went to school in Cottisford and then worked in Fringford. Her father worked on the rebuilding of Tusmore, she had cousins in Stoke Lyne, and her sister, May, lived in Hethe, where her mother died. No doubt there were many other similar family connections between the parishes.

Before the formation of the Shelswell Group Ministry in 1983, the following parishes had already been merged for administrative purposes. No doubt this was partly owing to the decline in church attendance and the shortage of clergy.

c.1840 Tusmore united with Hardwick.

1867 Charles Harrison became rector of Hardwick-with-Tusmore and Cottisford.

1924 Archdeacon Whylock Pendavis became rector of Hethe and Fringford.

1928 Godington united with Stratton Audley.

1932 Shelswell united with Newton Purcell.

1954 John Westlake became rector of Newton Purcell and Fringford.

1968-78 John Sergeant was rector of Newton Purcell, with responsibility for Fringford, Hethe, Cottisford and Hardwick-with-Tusmore.

1976 Anthony Hichens appointed priest-in-charge of Stratton Audley, Godington, Stoke Lyne, and Finmere with Mixbury.

1978 Donald Allan appointed priest-in-charge of Finmere-with-Mixbury, and together with Anthony Hichens looked after the ten parishes.

Donald Allan's appointment followed the retirement of John Sergeant. Sorting out how the ten parishes were to be run resulted in arguments and correspondence covering nearly five years. The new Northern and Southern Benefices eventually came into effect on 1 March 1983. Within six months Donald Allan left to take up a post in Essex and was replaced by Ronald Jennison.[5] When he retired in 1992, he was replaced by Warwick (Ricky) Yates. He became the first rector of the newly created ten-parish Benefice of Shelswell on 1 December 1995, after Anthony Hichens retired as rector of the Southern parishes. Ricky Yates departed at the end of August 2008 and his successor is yet to be appointed.

The first experiment with a group ministry in England was in 1949 in South Ormesby, Lincolnshire. As Trevor Beeson describes in his fine book *Round the Church in 50 Years: A Personal Journey*, 15 parishes, with 12 churches and a population of about 1,100, were merged. 'The rector, two curates, a deaconess and a lay reader were located strategically in different parishes in order to be able to travel easily to conduct services and to undertake pastoral work' Following this merger, 'The group ministry came to be seen as the answer to most of the church's rural problems and a large number of them were formed in every part of the country. It was believed that these group ministries would lead to a revival of rural church life but it was not foreseen that a serious reduction in the size of the ordained ministry would not allow them to be provided with South Ormesby scale resources. By the end of the century the Group had one priest – a woman.'[6]

The Shelswell Group was established along the same lines and has suffered to a lesser degree from the same lack of resources. At one time each of the ten parishes had their own resident rector, who was often a very powerful individual. Fringford, for example, had three wealthy and powerful rectors from 1814 to 1894. The parish benefited enormously from all three of them but the bishop himself could have done little if any of them had been a disaster. The parish too has been a very powerful unit and in many ways still is, in spite of the creation of a group ministry and then a benefice. The natural strength and independence of the parish units does give rise to problems. The parishes all know what services they like and are ready to demand a fair and equal share of the resources available. However, this does not mean that the services provided are all well attended. Before we look at today's attendance, it is time to examine the results of the 1851 Religious Census.

The religious census 1851 [7]

The religious census taken on Sunday 30 March 1851 was the first and only exercise of its kind ever carried out. Table 1 shows the results for the ten parishes in the Shelswell Benefice, including Lark Rise and its surrounding villages. Total attendance was 1,849, of whom 1,313 attended Church of England services, 386 Wesleyan Methodist ones and 150 the Roman Catholic mass. If we take a simple reading of the figures, attendance represented 58.9% of the population of the ten parishes, which totalled 3,140 (Table 7). Significantly, 30% of the attendance was at the Methodist and Roman Catholic chapels, with only 39% attending Church of England services. However, this does not take into account the number of people attending morning and afternoon services and the possible number of Wesleyans attending other services. If we assume that half of those attending morning service, i.e. 280, also attended afternoon service, this would reduce total attendance to 1,033 or 33%. This is more in line with the overall results for England and Wales, which showed that only some 50% of the population attended a service and, even worse, of them some 50% were Dissenters: i.e. only 25% of the population attended a Church of England service. As Bishop Wilberforce of Oxford had predicted, these results were a disaster for the Church of England.

Church services and attendance

It is interesting to take Fringford as a measure of the number and type of services held in the parishes in the nineteenth century. For the first half of the century, there were no more than 12 communion services per annum. By the 1850s this had increased to include Great Festivals and by the 1890s there was a communion service held every Sunday and on Holy Days. The overall number of services had also increased significantly by 1850, with two services on Sundays and Holy Days, a daily service at 8.30am and evening services on Wednesdays and Fridays. The average congregation was about 150 out of a population of 357.[8] The results of the

Table 1   Religious Census 30 March 1851
Shelswell Parishes

Parish	Church/Chapel	Date of Building	am	pm	evening	
			Services			
Cottisford	Parish Church		30	80		
			SS 40	SS 20		Note 1
Juniper Hill	Methodist	Cottage			30	Note 2
Finmere		Parish Church		220	220	
Fringford	Parish Church	C12-13	150	150		Note 3
		Independent Chapel		30	63	Note 4
Godington	Trinity Church	1792		50		
Hardwick-with-				SS 5		
Tusmore	Parish Church	Pre-1800		39		
				SS 10		
Hethe	Parish Church	Pre-1800	70	100		
			SS 30	SS 30		
	Catholic Chapel	1832	150			
	Methodist	1814	30	60	50	
			SS 25	SS 30		
Mixbury						Note 3
Newton Purcell-						
with-Shelswell	Parish Church		45	44		
			SS 20	SS 16		Note 5
Stoke Lyne	Established Church			30		Note 3
	Methodist	Cottage		68		
Stratton Audley	Established Church		40	40		Note 3
Total Attendance			**735**	**911**	**143**	

	am	pm	evening	Total
Church of England	560	753		1,313
Nonconformist/Catholic	205	188	143	536
	735	911	143	1,849

Notes

1 SS = Sunday Scholars

2 Juniper Hill is part of Cottisford parish but the information was provided by Thomas Lavine. He was tenant of the cottage where the Methodists met.

3 The clergymen in the following villages refused to answer the questions in the Census: Fringford, Mixbury, Stoke Lyne and Stratton Audley. Any answers were provided by the registrar or someone on his behalf.

4 There is no evidence that there was ever an Independent Chapel in Fringford. It also seems highly unlikely that there was ever such a gathering of Independents in the village.

5 Many of the boys usually attending the Sunday School were about in the fields bird-keeping.

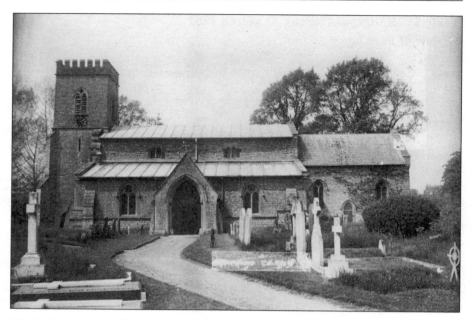

Fringford (Candleford Green) Church, where Flora heard the inspiring sermons of the Revd Charles Thompson (Mr Delafield), c.1920. (OCC)

Religious Census taken on 31 March 1851 bear this out. Table 1 shows the results for all the Shelswell parishes, including attendance at the Methodist and Roman Catholic chapels.

In Oxfordshire, it was not until 1866 that a marked change was evident in the number of daily and communion services. By then many villages were reporting services daily or once or twice a week, in addition to the observance of Holy Days and special seasons. Attendance seems to have been variable but overall on the increase. By 1899 Fringford reported attendance as 'very satisfactory'. There seems to have been 'a surprising steadiness of church and chapel life' in the country parishes in this period, as Owen Chadwick also found in Lincolnshire.[9]

In Fringford, when Flora arrived in 1891, 'a clergyman of the old type held the cure of souls of its inhabitants.' This was the Revd Cadwallader Coker (Mr Coulsdon) (1873-94). 'The services were long, old-fashioned and dull, but all was done decently and in order, and the music and singing were exceptionally good for a village church at that date. Mr Coulsdon preached to his poorer parishioners contentment with their divinely appointed lot in life and submission to the established order of earthly things.'[10] The Revd Charles Harrison (Mr Ellison) was doing just the same in Cottisford. After Coker's death in 1894, the new order arrived in

Fringford Ladies Cricket XI, postcard c.1915. Agnes Plumb, daughter of Frederick Plumb (Matthew), is sitting in the front row on the right. (Bill Plumb)

Fringford in the person of the Revd Charles Thompson (Mr Delafield) (1894-8). 'He soon won the 'reputation of being the best preacher in the neighbourhood – some said in the county.' As a parishioner was heard to say 'A sermon like that makes you feel two inches taller.'

Not only that but his arrival 'did as much as anything to hasten the decline of the old servile attitude of the poorer villagers.' 'Dignity did not enter into his composition. He would run out to post a letter in his shirtsleeves and, even when fully dressed, the only evidence of his sacred calling was his collar.' He had a charming way of relieving any old woman he met of any burden she was carrying, like a faggot of sticks or a clothesbasket of washing. Candleford Green cricket was put upon a proper footing and he got together a club for boys which met in the schoolroom on winter evenings.[11] Cricket has flourished at Fringford ever since then and there was also a Ladies Cricket XI by about 1915.

There was little change, however, in the nineteenth-century pattern of services until the 1960s. By then there was a 'torrent of proposals for change', as described vividly by Trevor Beeson. The 1960s was 'a stimulating and encouraging decade for reformers'. But by the end of the decade it was clear that 'optimism about the church's willingness to change, or even its ability to change, had been misplaced'. The Alternative Service Book (ASB), published in 1980, was the first authorized alternative to the

1662 Book of Common Prayer. The ASB was too large to be easily manageable and, as one report commented, 'the placing of a volume of 1,300 pages in the hands of a worshipper was a symptom of the gulf between the church and ordinary people'. The ASB was succeeded by a library of six books, including *Common Worship*, published in 2000. However, this contained so many variants that a number of booklets for use at particular services was also required. As Beeson concludes, 'No other church on earth ever elected to have wider variety or greater complexity in its forms of worship – not even those without liturgical texts.'[12]

Times have changed enormously since the 1851 census and the total population of the ten parishes has declined from 3,140 (Table 7) in 1851 to 2,560 in 2001. It is interesting to compare the latest figures available from the Oxford Diocese for church attendance, those for 2006 (Table 2). It no longer makes sense to compare individual parishes, as services are allocated on a group basis. The highest total attendance (516) was for the Harvest Festivals in early October, followed by Christmas Day (330) and Christmas Communion (303). These figures represent 20%, 13% and 12% respectively of the total population of 2,560. This is a significant decline and it does not take into account that the attendance in the other weeks in October 2006 was nearer the 100 mark. This is very similar to the number on the parish electoral rolls (106).

Apart from the new complexity of booklets, another major change has been the concentration on communion or eucharist services. This may please many but for others the loss of the traditional Prayer Book services and their beautiful language has been keenly felt. Another totally unexpected development has been the serious decline in the church's numerical strength. In spite of all these negative factors, Beeson's heroes are the parish priests who have kept the show on the road, ably assisted by over 2000 women in the priesthood and numerous lay-people. For the future he sees the need for a different structure. 'Let the parishes nominate their own priest to serve within a predominantly lay ministerial community. Such communities may well require, however, certain gifts that are not to be found within their own membership. These should be provided by a diocesan ministerial team, perhaps 100 strong, of full-time priests and lay specialists who, under the direction of the bishop, will be available to the parishes for tasks such as the ordering of worship, education, youth work and particular pastoral problems.'[13]

With declining church attendance and a shortage of clergy in the Shelswell Group, it is becoming increasingly difficult for the benefice to

Table 2   Church Attendance 2006
Shelswell Parishes

Parish	Popul'n 2001	Oct -06 Week 1 (Note 1)	Oct-06 Week 3 (Note 2)	Easter Day	Christmas Comm'n	Day
Cottisford	156	52	46	28	30	48
Finmere	436	87	12	34	37	51
Fringford	613	110	17	29	47	46
Godington (Note 3)	40					
Hardwick-with-Tusmore (Note 4)	53					
Hethe	279	38		24	37	25
Mixbury	255	90		42	67	68
Newton Purcell-with-Shelswell	103	6	8	4	4	6
Stoke Lyne	232	49		21	32	25
Stratton Audley	393	84	17	34	49	61
Total	2,560	516	100	216	303	330

Notes
1. Week 1 was the week of Harvest Festivals, so attendance was high.
2. Services are arranged on a Group basis, so there is not a service in every parish every Sunday.
3. Godington is included with Stratton Audley.
4. Hardwick-with-Tusmore is included with Cottisford.

maintain and service ten churches and for all the parishes to pay their shares to the Diocese. As Beeson says, there is a vital need for a new strategy. This may well include more services taken by lay people and more of them held in private houses.

Nonconformists

As we noted above, some 30% of the Group's attendance in March 1851 was at the Methodist and Roman Catholic chapels. Table 1 shows the significant Methodist presence in the Shelswell parishes, where 140 attended the three services in Hethe, 68 the evening service in Stoke Lyne, and 30 the evening service in Juniper Hill. These figures should not surprise us, as it was the Banbury district of Oxfordshire, just to the north, where the 1851 Census recorded by far the largest number of sittings available for Dissenters (44.29%). This contrasts with the figures for Oxfordshire as a whole, where Anglicanism was dominant as you would

Hethe Methodist Chapel, built in 1876, postcard early 1960s. (Mary Morgan)

expect in a traditional agricultural county, with 67.2% of the sittings Anglican and only 32.8% Dissenting. It is also worth noting that there were a number of villages just outside the Shelswell area with a strong Nonconformist presence, for example Fritwell and the Heyfords. In Fritwell there is still an active Methodist congregation.

Flora Thompson has left a vivid account of the services in Lark Rise, which were held in Thomas Lavine's cottage for a group of Primitive Methodists or 'Ranters'. Her father, Albert Timms, disapproved of them and only let Flora attend occasionally. Cottisford also disapproved of them, as shown by the rector's comment in 1860 that 'the greatest unity prevails from almost the absence of dissent'. The Methodists in Juniper Hill and Stoke Lyne never built a chapel and their meetings seem to have been short lived. In Stoke Lyne by the 1860s, there were only 15 'thorough-going dissenters', and it seems unlikely that the Ranters in Juniper survived as a group beyond 1900. However, Flora could still write of them in the 1880s, that 'Provided they did not attempt to convert others, religion in them was tolerated.'[14] She also wrote memorably of Methodism, that it was 'a people's religion, simple and crude; but its adherents brought to it more fervour than was shown by the church congregation, and appeared to obtain more comfort and support from it than the church could give. Their lives were exemplary.'[15]

In Hethe the earliest record of Free Church worship is 1794, when the Bishop of Oxford licensed the house of Mr Heydon, a shoemaker, for nonconformist meetings. The Heydon family were originally Presbyterians but we soon find them joining forces with the Methodists.

Other houses were licensed in 1810, 1816 and 1829. The first Methodist chapel was built in 1854 and a new one in 1876.[16] This did not close until the late 1960s and Mary Morgan recalls that Mr Cotton, the lay minister, continued to hold services for a few families in his home. She also remembers attending the annual Harvest Festival in the chapel and visits by the Brackley Methodist ladies every Good Friday for tea and a service. The old chapel is now a dwelling house.

Although the 1851 Census records a service at an Independent chapel in Fringford, there is no other evidence that there was ever a chapel in Fringford. It seems highly unlikely that there was ever such a gathering of Independents in the village. There is evidence of three dissenting families living in the village but the powerful Revd Henry Roundell actively discouraged any dissent. The census figures, which were provided by Thomas Freeman, local preacher, Launton, seem to be a simple mistake or misallocation.

Roman Catholics[17]

In the eighteenth and early nineteenth centuries, a number of Catholic communities survived in the area, in particular at Tusmore-with-Hardwick, Somerton and Souldern. The Fermor family, who were noted Catholics, owned Tusmore from the early seventeenth century until it was sold to Henry Howard, the 2nd Earl of Effingham, in 1857. There was a resident priest at Tusmore until 1810, when the house was let. At that point the chapel furniture was moved to the Old Manor House (now Manor Farm) in Hardwick, where a chapel was made in the barrel vaulted attic, which ran the whole length of the house. It seems clear that Catholic recusants had assembled here long before this, probably since the late sixteenth century.

The Old Manor House had been let by the Fermors throughout the eighteenth century, and latterly was occupied by the Day family until 1793. They were succeeded by their relatives the Collingridges, who remained until 1812. It seems that the local Catholics were gathering here about once a month, and in 1810 Father Samuel Corbishley took charge of the Mission. He was a very strict and austere priest and he lived in Hardwick until his death in 1830, serving a flock of some 350, and also keeping a small school. In 1823, the 'greatest part' of the inhabitants of Hardwick, 78 out of 98, were still Catholic, but by 1854 under half of the population were.

In 1830 immediately after Father Corbishley's death, the Hardwick manor house was closed to Catholics and Father Alfred McGuire was appointed. He lived in Hethe and initially celebrated mass in various houses in the village. He rapidly bought land and organised subscriptions for a new chapel, Holy Trinity, which was opened on 22 May 1832 and continues to flourish to this day. He clearly had strong support from a number of local families, particularly the Collingridges, of whom some fifty were confirmed as Catholics at Hardwick and Tusmore in the last quarter of the eighteenth century. Many of them were born at Pimlico Farm, near Tusmore, and members of the family also lived at Hethe, Fritwell, Godington, and Somerton.

At least four members of the family went into the church, with Peter (1757-1829) becoming a prominent Franciscan, and Vicar Apostolic of the Western District, comprising Wales and the whole south-west of England. Alfred 'the Zouave' (1846-67) was born at Moat Farm, Godington, where there was a chapel in the roof, only dismantled in about 1900. He moved to France with his parents and joined the Jesuits. He then answered the call of Pope Pius IX to defend the Papal States against Garibaldi and joined the 'Pontifical Zouaves', who were crack units of the French army. Corporal Alfred was killed at the battle of Mertana in Italy in 1867.

In 1851 there were only eight places of worship for the Roman Catholics in Oxfordshire. In Hethe, however, the strong Catholic tradition continued and attendance of 150 at morning service was the norm. In Lark Rise, as Flora recalled, 'The Catholic minority at the inn was treated with respect, for a landlord could do no wrong, especially the landlord of a free house where such excellent beer was on tap.' 'When, early in life, the end house children asked what Roman Catholics were, they were told

Hethe Roman Catholic Chapel, built in 1832, postcard early 1960s. (Mary Morgan)

that they were "folks as prays to images", and that 'they worshipped the Pope, a bad old man, some said in league with the Devil.' 'Yet the children's grandfather, when the sound of the Angelus bell was borne on the wind from the chapel in the next village, would take off his hat and, after a moment's silence, murmur, "In my Father's house are many mansions." It was all very puzzling.'[18]

Holy Trinity Church continued to serve Hethe on its own until 1984, during which time the Catholic congregation varied from 80 to 110. In 1984 Adderbury was joined to Hethe to create the new parish of Hethe-with-Adderbury. Today Holy Trinity continues to prosper with a joint congregation of 130-150. In 2007 I was privileged to attend a fine service to celebrate its 175th anniversary. It should also be said that the Hethe Christmas carol service alternates between the Anglican and Catholic churches. Will the future bring further unity, both within the Church of England, and with the Nonconformists and Catholics?

Notes

1   Flora Thompson, *Lark Rise to Candleford*, 211.

2   Thompson, *Lark Rise*, 179.

3   Thompson, *Lark Rise*, 210.

4   Thompson, *Lark Rise*, 212.

5   Finmere and Little Tingewick Historical Society, *The Millennium History of Finmere*, 21.

6   Trevor Beeson, *Round the Church in 50 Years, An Intimate Journey*, 60.

7   Kate Tiller, *Church and Chapel in Oxfordshire 1851: The return of the census of religious worship*, The Oxfordshire Record Society 55, 1987.

8   M.W. Greenwood, *Parishes, Parsons and Persuasions*, 24.

9   Owen Chadwick, *The Victorian Church*, Part Two, 1860-1901, 159.

10   Thompson, *Lark Rise*, 424-6.

11   Thompson, *Lark Rise*, 523-8.

12   Beeson, *Round the Church*, 66.

13   Beeson, *Round the Church*, 278.

14   Thompson, *Lark Rise*, 215.

15   Thompson, *Lark Rise*, 219.

16   John M.Sergeant, *The Story of Hethe, Oxfordshire*, 14.

17   Joy Grant, *Hethe-with-Adderbury, The Story of a Catholic Parish in Oxfordshire*.

18   Thompson, *Lark Rise*, 213-4.

Chapter 3

The 'Great Houses'

'The old Earl was spoken of as "our Earl" and when the flag, flown
from the tower of his mansion to show he was in residence, could be
seen floating above tree-tops they would say:
"I see our family's at home again." '[1]

The Lark Rise people 'took a pride in their rich and powerful country-
house neighbours, especially when titled,' and 'by some inherited
instinct they felt that he [the Earl] belonged to them.'[2] There are a number
of large country houses within the Shelswell area, including Shelswell
Park, Swift's House and Tusmore Park, although none of them is strictly
a 'great house', like Blenheim or Stowe. However, they have been large
enough to have their own supporting communities, while still being dependent on the local villages for a variety of services. I examine how these
three 'great houses' were almost self-contained communities, while also
providing employment and housing for local inhabitants. There are
similar large, if not great, houses in some of the other villages, particularly
Stratton Audley, where we shall see their influence in the next chapter.

Shelswell Park

For many BBC viewers Shelswell Park will now be seen as the home of
'Sir Timothy' (Edward Slater-Harrison). There is no longer a 'great house',
as it fell into disrepair and was demolished in the late 1970s. However, the
fine stable block, which was gutted by fire in 1983, has been refurbished
and is now let as a private dwelling. It is still possible to walk through the
lovely park and admire the stable block. There used to be a medieval village
in Shelswell, with a manor house and St Ebbe's church, probably on a site
just across the river from the Old Rectory. However, enclosure and the
consequent depopulation were completed by 1601. In the early eighteenth
century, the Trotmans are said to have built a new manor house. In 1875
Edward Slater-Harrison pulled down nearly the whole of the house and

Shelswell House, view from the park, with the stable block on the right, 1901. (OCC)

built a new mansion, designed by the Oxford architect William Wilkinson. Edward died in 1911 but his second wife, Emma Cecilia (née Cartwright), continued to live here until her death in 1943.

We have already discussed Flora's description of her visit to meet 'Sir Timothy' and her memories of his first wife, 'Lady Adelaide'. She has also given a vivid description of the celebrations for Queen Victoria's Jubilee in 1887, which were held in 'Skeldon' (Shelswell) Park. She attended them with her mother Emma, and her brother Edwin, and sisters May and Elizabeth.[3] Flora has also given a glimpse of the excitement caused to the children by the rare sight of 'Squire Harrison's four-in-hand, with ladies in bright summer dresses, like a garden of flowers, on the top of the coach, and the Squire himself, pink-cheeked and white hatted, handling the four greys. When the four-in-hand passed, the children drew back and saluted, the Squire would gravely touch the brim of his hat with his whip, and the ladies would lean from their high seats to smile on the curtseying children.'[4]

Table 3   Shelswell Park
Domestic and Outdoor Staff

Year	1851 (Note 1)	1861	1871	1881	1891 (Note 2)	1901
Domestic Staff						
governess	1					
housekeeper		1	1	1		1
cook						1
lady's maid		2	1	1	1	2
house maid		2	2	2	2	3
kitchen maid		2	1	1	1	1
scullery maid			1	1	1	1
nurse maid			2			
butler		1	1	1		
footman		1	1	2		2
houseboy		1	1			
Total	13	10	11	9	5	11
Outdoor Staff						
stable man/groom		1			2	3
coachman						1
gardener	1	1	1	1	1	1
gamekeeper		1	1	1	1	1
farmer	2	2	2	2	2	2
shepherd		1		1		
land agent		1		1		
blacksmith			1			
ag.lab.	2		2	2	1	1
Total outdoor	5	7	7	8	7	9
Total	18	17	18	17	12	20
Total community	43	44	43	42	17	45

Notes
1. In 1851, the only servant given a title was the governess.
2. In 1891, the Slater-Harrisons were away.

Although there was no real village of Shelswell by the nineteenth century, the census returns from 1851 to 1901 do provide an interesting picture of the household at Shelswell and the size of the community (Table 3). In 1851 John and Louisa Slater-Harrison were resident with their children – Louisa (19), Edward (18) and Augusta (14), 13 domestics

Edward Slater-Harrison (Sir Timothy) with his coach & four outside Shelswell House, 1902. This is probably the coach on which Flora used to see the Squire. (OCC)

(four male, nine female) and five outdoor staff, and a total community of 43. The only servant given a title was Charlotte Hendre, the governess aged 30, from London. Only five of the domestic staff were born locally, while the outdoor staff and the farmers' six servants were all born within the local area. This is a recognised pattern, with the gentry often employing most of their servants from further afield, while the farmers tended to employ local people. In part, this was because the gentry feared that the locals might betray secrets of their households.

In 1861 and 1871 John and Louisa were in residence with a similar sized household and community. In 1861 they had 10 indoor servants (three male, seven female), five of them born locally, and seven outdoor staff (all local). In 1871 there were 11 indoor servants (three male, eight female), of whom only two were born locally, and seven outdoor staff (six local). From 1861 details of the servants employed are given, with the two most important being the housekeeper and the butler. 'These personages were regarded by the under-servants almost as kings and queens.'[5] The other staff included ladiesmaids, housemaids, nursemaids, kitchen and scullery maids, footmen and houseboys. The houses on the estate were homes to the two farmers, a gardener, gamekeeper, shepherd, and labourers.

John died in 1874 and in 1881 his son, Edward Slater-Harrison (Sir Timothy), was in residence with his first wife, Cecilia (Lady Adelaide). They had nine domestic servants (three male, six female), three of them born locally, eight outdoor staff (seven local), and a total community of 42. In 1891 the Slater-Harrisons were away but left a skeleton domestic staff of five (all female) and seven outdoor staff. Only two of the community of 17 were born locally. In 1901 Edward was in residence with his second wife, Emma Cecilia, with 11 domestic servants (two male, nine female), of whom only three were local. The nine outdoor staff (eight local) included two farmers at Home Farm and Newton Grange, a game-keeper, gardener, labourer, and John Stenton, the stationmaster at Finmere Station (see Chapter 6). The total community numbered 45.

Edward Slater-Harrison, who died in 1911, had no son and was succeeded by his nephew, Major Arthur William Dewar of Cotmore House, Fringford, on condition that he added the name 'Harrison' to his own. He was living in Hethe House, which had been built as a Dower House by the Trotman family of Shelswell, who owned Hethe in the eigh-teenth century. In 1913-14 he moved to the farmhouse at Willaston, where he died in 1923. He was succeeded by his second son, John Francis Dewar-Harrison, who was squire for 44 years from 1923 to 1967.

He moved to Shelswell House, which was still occupied by Emma Cecilia (née Cartwright), Edward's second wife, who lived on until 1943. 'She maintained Shelswell House in its ancient glory, with beautiful gardens, greenhouses, fishponds, watercress beds and a plant house with a thousand plants. She kept six full time gardeners and six housemaids, all of whom remember her for her motherly care, and was guarded by six fierce dogs.' During the Second World War, there was an airfield to the east of Shelswell Park, consisting of about eight fields, where the hedges were removed and replaced with irregular cinder tracks, which looked like hedges from the air. A maintenance unit was based there. Featherbed Lane was closed to traffic as bombs were stored there. Shelswell House was used to house RAF officers. After the war the house was converted into flats for local families. By the late 1970s it had become almost uninhabitable and was demolished. The surviving stable block was gutted by fire in 1983 but an excellent refurbishment was completed in 2000 and it is now rented as a private dwelling.

After the house was converted into flats, John Dewar-Harrison moved to Willaston, where he lived until his death in 1967. He is remembered for his care for the local village communities and for all the individuals in them, particularly in Fringford and Hethe. In an article in the *Bicester Advertiser* of 10 February 1967, one of his closest friends was quoted as having said 'He was the last of the Squires and Country Gentlemen'. On his death, the heavy incidence of death duties split up the estate. Houses and land were sold and several of his farms were left to his tenant farmers in return for payment of their share of the estate duty. The residue of his estate passed to his goddaughter, Lydia Ann Smith, later Baroness Ann

Swift's House, Stoke Lyne, in the 1950s. The top floor was removed c.1970. (Brenda Long)

von Maltzahn. She and her husband, who have three children, continue to live at Shelswell at The Home Farm House. [6]

Swift's House

In the early nineteenth century, Sir Thomas Mostyn, who earlier had moved from Flintshire to Bainton with his hounds (see Chapter 4), bought Swift's House, then a small alehouse, on the Bicester-Aynho Turnpike, near Baynards Green. 'He soon converted it into a very comfortable house for himself, and most complete accommodation for his hounds, horses, and servants.' 'The stables are uncommonly good and built to the form of a quadrangle, with the huntsman's house, kennel, blacksmith's shop etc, on the outside.'[7] He moved there with his hounds and supported the pack until his death in 1829. In 1830, Sir Henry Peyton (1765-1854), the 2nd Baronet, bought the house, and the Peyton family lived there until 1993. The family came from Cambridgeshire, where they held large landed property in Doddington.

In 1851 Sir Henry and his wife, Henrietta, were resident at Swift's House with 17 staff, of whom only four were born locally (Table 4). He was succeeded by Sir Henry Peyton the younger (1804-66), the 3rd Baronet. In 1861 the Peytons were away but they left a skeleton staff of seven, including three grooms, at Swift's House. Sir Henry was succeeded by his only surviving son, Sir Algernon (1833-72), the 4th Baronet. In 1871 he was living at Stratton Audley Hall with his wife, Laura, and 10

Table 4 Swift's House
Domestic and Outdoor Staff

Year	1851	1861 (Note 1)	1871 (Note 2)	1881	1891	1901
Domestic Staff						
butler	1			1	1	
housekeeper	1					
cook				1	1	1
lady's maid	3			4	2	3
nurse					1	1
house maid	2	1		2	3	2
kitchen maid	1				1	1
scullery maid	1			1		1
laundry maid				1		
houseboy	1	1			1	1
dairymaid	1					
under butler	1					
footman	1			2	1	1
Total domestic	13	2		12	11	11
Outdoor Staff						
gardener	1	1		2	2	1
coachman	1			1	2	1
groom	2	3		4	2	5
farm bailiff		1				
Total outdoor	4	5		7	6	7
Total	17	7		19	17	18

Notes
1. In 1861, the Peytons were away.
2. In 1871, Sir Algernon Peyton, 4th Bt., was living at Stratton Audley Hall, with his wife and 10 servants. He died in 1872. The only occupant at Swift's House was Joseph Busby (labourer) and his family at the Lodge.

servants. She was still living there in 1876. In 1871 the only resident at Swift's House was Joseph Busby (labourer) and his family at the Lodge. It is possible that the improvements to the house and gardens may have been started by then. Sir Algernon died suddenly in 1872, in the King's Arms, Bicester, after a day's hunting. He was succeeded by his cousin, Major-General Sir Thomas Peyton (1817-88), the 5th Baronet. In 1881 he and his wife, Lucy, were at Swift's House, with their daughter, Elizabeth (19), and 19 staff, of whom nine were born locally. The staff included a coachman and four grooms. It was Sir Thomas who 'greatly improved its

[Swift's] surroundings by turning the public road, which then ran close by the house where the present drive from its two entrances now runs, into its present position at a distance from the house, and planting the intervening space with ornamental shrubs and trees.'[8]

In 1891 and 1901 Sir Algernon (1855-1916), the 6th Baronet, and his wife, Ida, were at home, on each occasion with a large staff, 17 in 1891, and 18 in 1901. Only a third of them were born locally. In 1901, the staff included a coachman, a stud groom and four other grooms. Sir Algernon was succeeded by his son, also Sir Algernon (1889-1962), the 7th Baronet. Detailed records are not available for later years but it is safe to assume that the size of the household was considerably reduced after the Great War. During the Second World War the house was occupied as an evacuee centre (see Chapter 6). John, the only son of the 7th Baronet, was killed in the war, just before the German surrender on 4 May 1945 (see Chapter 7), and the family baronetcy became extinct. His sister, Delia, married Major Benjamin Barnett from Glympton. They lived at Swift's House until the late 1980s, when they sold land for the M40 services area at Baynard's Green and moved to Purston, near Banbury. Their elder son, David, with his wife, Annabel, lived at Swift's House after his parents left. In the late 1980s. In 1993 the link with the Peyton family was finally severed, when they sold Swift's House to Jim and Brenda Long.

Tusmore Park

As we have seen above (Chapter 2), the Fermors, a noted Catholic family, owned Tusmore Park from the early seventeenth century. In 1766 William Fermor built an elegant Grecian mansion, designed by Robert Mylne. He was frequently the host of Mrs Fitzherbert in the 1790s, and tradition has it that she married George IV at Tusmore.[9] After William's death in 1823, the house was leased until it was sold in 1857. The 1851 census gives some idea of the scale of the house and community. The Hon. Percy Barrington was leasing it and living there with his wife, two daughters and his son, 13 domestic servants and 10 outdoor staff (Table 5). The total community numbered 52, including two farmers. Joseph Eden was farming 560 acres with 16 labourers, and William Jones 150 acres with his brother, Josiah. In 1857 Henry Howard, the 2nd Earl of Effingham (1806-89), bought Tusmore. By then much of the house had been damaged by fire and the Earl made substantial improvements and alterations. It was then that Flora's father, Albert, 'helped to finish rebuilding that house.'[10] In 1861 the Earl was living there with his wife,

Tusmore Park, view across the lake, the home of the Earl of Effingham, 'our Earl', in Flora's day, 1912. (Wafic Said)

Eliza, and three children, 18 domestic servants (15 female, three male), and 12 outdoor staff. None of the domestic staff were born locally and only four of the outdoor staff. By any standards this was an impressive household and much grander than Shelswell Park or Swift's House. The total community of 45 included Thomas Berridge, aged 23, who was farming 610 acres at Pimlico Farm, and employing 20 men and boys, and six women. In 1871 the 2nd Earl and his wife were in residence, with two daughters and a grandson, 20 domestic servants (16 female, four male), of whom only two were local, and four outdoor staff. The community of 43 still included Thomas Berridge at Pimlico Farm, employing 40 men and boys. In 1872 the Earl's landed property in Oxfordshire was reckoned at 3,376 acres.

In 1881 the 2nd Earl and his wife were at 57, Eaton Place with a much smaller household, leaving a skeleton staff of 12 at Tusmore. Only four domestic staff were local. The total community of 27 was correspondingly smaller. In 1891 the 3rd Earl (d.1898) was not in residence but his son, Henry Howard, Lord Howard of Effingham, aged 24, was there with a skeleton staff of eight (five local) and a total community of 16. By 1901 he was the 4th Earl (1866-1927) but still a bachelor and in residence with only four domestic staff, and an outdoor staff of 10. Six of the staff were born locally. The total community of 51 included Daniel Ginger, who was farming with two of his sons, presumably at Pimlico Farm.

After the death of the 4th Earl, the house was sold in 1929 to Vivian Hugh Smith, created Lord Bicester of Tusmore in 1938. His father had been Governor of the Bank of England and he was an outstanding business man, Lord Lieutenant of Oxfordshire (1934-56), and a well-known race-horse owner, as we shall see below (Chapter 4). He remodelled the house, adding formal gardens, in the 1930s. During the Second World War, Tusmore was converted into an Auxiliary Hospital, organised by the Red Cross and the Order of St. John of Jerusalem, for Army, Navy and Air Force wounded. Some 80 patients for long-term care were there following head injury operations at St. Hugh's College, Oxford. Lord and Lady Bicester continued to live at Tusmore with a limited staff in a ground floor flat, and were extremely generous to the young men injured. There were similar conversions to hospitals or convalescent homes in a number of local villages, for example Audley End in Chesterton, Fritwell Manor, and Middleton Stoney Park.

The Commandant of the Tusmore hospital was Miss Joyce Tomkinson of Fringford. She was very sporty, playing tennis and ping-pong with the patients and staff. She was a great character and, after the war, played a leading part in village life in Fringford, where she was greatly loved and

'Somewhere in Oxfordshire': nurses at Tusmore Park during the Second World War, *The Queen*, February, 1942. (Nurse Curran's family)

Table 5   Tusmore Park
Domestic and Outdoor Staff

Year	1851	1861	1871	1881 (Note 1)	1891 (Note 2)	1901 (Note 3)
Domestic Staff						
butler	1	1	1			1
footman	1	2	2			
governess	1					
housekeeper	1	1	1			
nurse/nursemaid	2		1			
lady's maid	1	2	2			
house maid	2	4	3	2		2
needlewoman	1					
cook		1	1			1
kitchen maid		1	1			
scullery maid		1	1			
dairymaid		1	1	1		
still room maid	1	1	1			
laundry maid		3	4	3		
valet	1					
errand boy	1			1		
page			1			
domestic servant					3	
Total domestic	13	18	20	7	3	4
Outdoor Staff						
coachman	1	1	1			1
groom	2	2				
stable man		1				
gamekeeper	1				1	1
gardener				1	1	1
bailiff/steward		2	1	1		1
farmer	2	1	1	1	1	1
carter		2	1		1	2
shepherd		2				1
clerk of works		1				
ag.lab.	2			2	1	1
ag.oddman	1					1
lacemaker	1					
Total outdoor	10	12	4	5	5	10
Total	23	30	24	12	8	14
Total community	52	45	43	27	16	51

Notes
1. In 1881, the 2nd Earl and his wife were at 57 Eaton Place, London.
2. In 1891, the 3rd Earl was not in residence.
3. In 1901, the bachelor 4th Earl was in residence.

War Service Award to Joan Coles (née Staniforth) for nursing at Tusmore Park. (Joan Staniforth)

a little feared by the village. She was a very keen horsewoman, riding side-saddle to hounds, and never missing a meet until a few months before her death. A number of the nurses and auxiliaries were extremely well connected, including Lady Anne Fitzroy, daughter of the Duke of Grafton, Lavinia Lascelles, daughter of Sir Alan Lascelles, Private Secretary to the King, and Delia Holland-Hibbert, niece of Viscount Knutsford. As Joan Staniforth (née Coles), one of the nurses, recalls, there were a number of visits from the Royal Family, including Queen Mary, the Queen Mother, and the Earl and Countess Mountbatten. Lady Bicester's mother, the Countess of Antrim, who was Lady-in–Waiting to Queen Mary, also visited. Joan, who still lives in Brackley, remembers her time at Tusmore vividly and has many happy memories.

She, like others, used to cycle in before dawn to be on duty by 6.00 am. On one dark morning, she was aware of a huge dark shape coming towards her. Her first thought was that it must be a large army vehicle. On getting closer, she realised to her amazement that it was an elephant and she took evasive action in the ditch. The minder assured her that it would not harm her and told her that he was transferring it from Bicester to Brackley station. Who knows where the elephant had come from and where it was going to! Needless to say, Joan had a hard time convincing others what she had seen, until she showed them the marker which the elephant had conveniently left just outside the main gates! After the war, Joan, like the other nurses and auxiliaries, received a certificate (see above) from the War Organisation of the Order of the Red Cross Society and Order of St John of Jerusalem 'in recognition of devoted service to the cause of humanity during the second world war 1939-1945'. She continues to keep in touch with a few of her nursing friends from those days.

Lord Bicester died in 1956 and was succeeded by his son, Randal, the 2nd Lord Bicester. He demolished the house in 1961, and replaced it with a new house, designed by Claude Phillimore. For a variety of reasons the design was not a success. Indeed, it was described later by the architect of the new house as 'a deeply dispiriting house'. In particular, the exterior stone came from the wrong quarry and turned a horrible orange colour, clashing with the Georgian stables and other retained outbuildings. Randal was killed in a car accident on 'Smith-Bingham Corner' in Newton Morrell in 1968. The title passed to his nephew, who sadly has spent much of his life in psychiatric institutions. In his absence, Tusmore was occupied for many years by the 2nd Lord Bicester's daughter, Mrs John Collins and her husband. In 1987, the estate was sold to Wafic Said, the main sponsor of the Said Business School of Oxford University, who demolished the house. He then built the new Tusmore Park, 'the finest Classical house built in Britain since the Second World War, and perhaps the grandest since Manderston in Berwickshire, in the Edwardian age.'[11] It was built with a beautiful creamy Messengis stone from Burgundy, which is closely comparable to a Cotswold stone.

Servants

It is possible to put the number of staff in these great houses in some perspective. In 1851 there were 751,000 females in domestic service in England and Wales. This had risen to 1,285,000 by 1901. The number in 1911 was still very similar, when there were some 800,000 families with servants.[12] During the Great War, the number of female domestics fell by a quarter, while female munitions workers increased from 212,000 to over 900,000. By 1921, the number of women and girls in service had recovered to about 1.2 million, after the war-time decline. In the 1920s, however, the economic depression and the growth of unemployment saw more girls reluctantly forced into service. By 1931, there were 1.3 million female servants, of whom 1.1 million were in private service, although many of the girls were much more reluctant to accept subordinate status. By 1951, this attitude was much more prevalent and there were only some 350,000 women in private domestic service. By 1969, the total number had shrunk to 106,000.[13]

As we have seen, in the second half of the nineteenth century the local 'great houses' all required a significant number of domestic and outdoor staff. Most of them were not recruited locally. The diary of the Revd W.C. Risley, vicar of Deddington (1836-48), sheds some interesting light on the possible reasons for this. He rejected a candidate for the post of footman purely on the grounds that he had 'friends living in the Place'. Similarly, a former servant from the Ewelme area of Oxfordshire recalled that it was usual for youngsters in her parish to be sent at least twenty miles away from home – 'probably to discourage followers or to stop the girls running home'.[14]

By contrast, if you look at the households of the Fringford farmers, for example Cotmore and Waterloo, many of their servants were recruited from the local villages. However, if you were ambitious, the great houses provided much greater scope for advancement. That said, sooner or later most youngsters from the country districts, particularly the girls, would have to move away to the towns, since it was here (especially in London) that the bulk of the vacancies for servants lay. The end of the century also saw the growing reluctance of girls to enter service and the emergence of 'servant shortages', which 'became a menace' according to one member of the upper class![15]

Although there are no records available for the local great houses after 1901, the size of their estates and households certainly reduced, particularly during and after the Great War. However, the need for indoor and outdoor servants continued both for them and the local farmers, even if there may now have been more emphasis on daily help from the local villages. The great houses also still needed help to run and maintain their estates, so that they continued to provide work for local builders, plumbers, electricians, butchers and other services and suppliers. All the Shelswell villages would have benefited, and indeed still benefit to a lesser extent, from this patronage, as do the local towns, Bicester, Banbury and Brackley. As we see in the next chapter, the great houses also helped local employment by their support of the Bicester Hunt.

The influence of the great houses has also extended to housing, which has been provided for staff at Shelswell, Swift's House and Tusmore; in Fringford too, where John Dewar-Harrison converted the Manor in 1948 into houses for some of his workers on the Shelswell estate. It had proved impossible to build new houses for them because of shortages after the war. The great houses have also owned most of the local farms, which have been worked by tenant farmers. As we have seen, John Dewar-Harrison again showed his generosity by leaving his farms to the tenants provided they paid their share of the estate duty.

Notes

1   Flora Thompson, *Lark Rise to Candleford*, 289.
2   Thompson, *Lark Rise*, 290.
3   Thompson, *Lark Rise*, 242-6.
4   Thompson, *Lark Rise*, 174.
5   Pamela Horn, *The Rise and Fall of the Victorian Servant*, 24.
6   John M. Sergeant, *The Story of Hethe, Oxfordshire*, 15.
7   Ralph Greaves, *A Short History of the Bicester & Warden Hill Hunt*, quoting *Nimrod*, 13.
8   J.C. Blomfield, *Deanery of Bicester,* Part VIII, 27.
9   Blomfield, *Deanery of Bicester*, Part III, 83.
10 Christine Bloxham, *The World of Flora Thompson Revisited*, 102.
11 *Country Life*, December 8, 2005, 51.
12 Horn, *Rise and Fall*, 190 and 231.
13 Horn, *Rise and* Fall, 202.
14 Horn, *Rise and Fall*, 36.
15 Paul Thompson, *The Edwardians: The Remaking of British Society*, 95.

Chapter 4

'The Chase and the Turf'

'A district studded with Gentlemen's seats and Hunting Boxes,
affording society of the most agreeable kind.'[1]

When Tusmore House was sold to the 2nd Earl of Effingham in 1857,
the advertisement included this glowing testimonial to the hunting
boxes and the agreeable society in the district. The Peyton family of Swift's
House was a significant part of this agreeable society and it was said of
them that they were 'much identified with the Chase, the Turf and the
Road.'[2] The same could be said of a great many other local families.
'Nothing gave a gentleman greater prestige in his county, which was what
most of them cared about, than riding hard to hounds.'[3] In 1844, when
Cottisford Manor Farm was sold, the Sale Catalogue mentioned the
hunting potential: 'Good hunting is available in the immediate district,
being in the heart of the Bicester country and within easy reach of the
Grafton, Heythrop and Whaddon Chase hunts.'[4] As a keen older supporter
recalled, the riders never noticed county boundaries, only the borders of the
hunting countries. When John Betjeman toured this part of England in the
1930s, he commented ' "Bicestershire", the smart hunting district, special
train to London in the mornings, hearty after-hunting breakfast, first-class
passengers, first-class fences, foxes in every covert, rain always.'[5]

The Bicester Hunt[6]

Hunting has had a significant influence on the district for some two
hundred and fifty years or more. The Bicester and Warden Hill Hunt goes
back to 1778, when John Warde, 'the Father of Hunting' and a celebrated
rider to hounds, kept a pack of hounds at Weston-on-the-Green and
hunted a large area in Warwickshire and Oxfordshire. By 1783 he was
using Bainton Manor Farm as a hunting box. Since then the Hunt kennels
have always been sited within the Shelswell area, first at Bainton, then
Swift's House, and now at Stratton Audley.

Bainton Manor

John Warde and Joseph Bullock of Caversfield, who had bought Bainton Manor, co-operated in building stables and kennels there. By 1800 Sir Thomas Mostyn of Mostyn Hall in Flintshire was living at Bainton, with the Mostyn Hounds, which became known as the Bicester Hounds. He continued to travel frequently between Flintshire and Bicester. He had a hound named 'Lady', who was a great favourite of his and during his journeys she accompanied him, walking by the side of his carriage. During one of his visits to the kennel, he asked the kennel man to be sure to keep Lady shut in, as she was due to have puppies and he did not want her to travel back to Wales with him. A few days later, however, Lady got out and disappeared. Sometime later she arrived at Rewl Mostyn, tired and hungry, having given birth to her puppies. After feeding her she was followed some miles to where she had left her puppies safely nestling in a bed of bracken in a shallow ditch. They were carried back and her puppies became the foundation of the nineteenth-century Bicester pack. In 1812 Mostyn erected a large obelisk 'In Memory of his favourite hound Lady', which still stands at Bainton where she died.[7]

Swift's House

As we have seen above, Sir Thomas Mostyn built Swift's House in the early nineteenth century, and moved there with his hounds and supported the pack until his death in 1829. He was joined at Swift's House by the Revd Griff Lloyd, who was a Fellow of All Souls, and rector of Christleton, near Chester. At the same time he managed to get himself appointed curate of Newton Purcell (1805-43) and he was given a licence to live with Mostyn to 'look after his cousin's hounds and morals'! He lived with him, 'most of the season, going backwards and forwards to Christleton by coach, to perform his duties, which, however, he never allowed to clash with hunting days.' Griff, who appeared in Punch cartoons, was nationally famous as the 'The Hunting Parson' or more popularly as 'The Black Whipper-In'.[8]

Mostyn gave prizes for the Farmers' Cup Race, which was run at Northbrook, near Kirtlington, until the field was enclosed, then on Cottisford Heath. The races were still running outside Juniper Hill near the 'turnpike' (A43) in 1827. *The Times* of 31 March 1826 reported on the Mostyn Hunt Races, where 'the assemblage of fashionables were very great, and included Earl Jersey, Sir Thomas Mostyn, Sir Edward Mostyn, Sir H.Peyton, George Mostyn, Esq., and most of the members of the hunt.' The races used to be run at 'the end of March or early April, the last hunting day but one of the season', like the modern Point-to-Points at Mollington and elsewhere. Blomfield gives a vivid account of these races: 'the Farmers' Cup Race, for horses, not thoroughbred, that had regularly hunted with the packs of the Duke of Grafton or Beaufort, or that of Sir Thomas Mostyn, to be ridden by the owners or friendly non-professional riders. This was the great attraction of the day, at least to the agricultural eye…'. [9] John Harrison of Shelswell Park (1781-1834), who was a great sportsman and jockey, frequently won races here in the early 1800s.

In 1830 Sir Henry Peyton (1765-1854), the 2nd Baronet, bought the house. It was described then as a 'Capital Hunting Residence, with convenient offices, excellent stables for 24 horses besides boxes, kennels, keeper's lodge, garden, yards and 60 acres of grass and arable land.' Sir Henry and his family were well known as gentlemen coach-drivers, and later members of the family were 'much identified with the Chase, the Turf and the Road.' It should also be said that the family's hunting connection went back much further, as Sir Sewster Peyton was Master of the Buckhounds to Queen Anne. Sir Henry drove a yellow coach with four gray horses and was a familiar sight driving slowly through the streets of Mayfair and Belgravia or around Oxfordshire, 'his coach laden with a party of hunting men, on its way to the fixture of Mr Drake's hounds.' [10]

Sir Henry Peyton the younger (1804-66), the 3rd Baronet, also drove the yellow coach with four grays. He was one of the best cross-country riders in England and a noted hunting man. Sir Algernon, the 4th Baronet, was master in 1862-63 and 1870-72. He died suddenly in 1872, in the King's Arms, Bicester, after a days' hunting. Sir Thomas (1817-88), the 5th Baronet, was also 'passionately fond of driving his four-in-hand coach, and for some years during the London season he drove the Windsor Coach daily.' [11] He could also be seen riding beside Baron Deichmann of The Garth, Bicester, who was another enthusiast for four-in-hand coaching from the 1880s. Many other distinguished people were to be seen riding beside him, including the Duke of Beaufort, the Earl of Jersey, and Edward Slater-Harrison. The 6th and 7th Baronets were both keen followers of the Hunt. The family connection with 'the Turf' also lives on with one of the 7th Baronet's grandsons, Charles Barnett, who runs the Ascot Racecourse, having previously run Aintree.

Stratton Audley

Stratton Audley became the centre of the Bicester and Warden Hill Hunt when Tom Tyrwhitt-Drake took over the hounds in 1851. His father, who was MP for Amersham, lived locally at Bucknell and had been master from 1829-51 in succession to Mostyn. Tom was master for most of the period 1851 to 1866. By 1852, he had bought the Old Rectory (now Stratton Audley Hall), and converted it to a full hunting establishment, with stabling and kennels, where the hounds have since remained. In 1861, Drake was living there with his wife, five daughters, four sons, a governess and 15 domestic servants! Drake was succeeded as master by Lord North of Wroxton Abbey, who brought his own pack of hounds to Stratton Audley, also buying the pick of Drake's hounds. He gave up the country in 1870, owing to ill-health.

Between 1872 and 1893 there were two other well-known masters, Arthur Annesley, the 11th Viscount Valentia (1872-84) and Charles Compton William Cavendish, the 3rd Lord Chesham (1884-93), who successively rented Stratton Audley Hall. Viscount Valentia was MP for Oxford (1895-1917) and Comptroller of the Royal Household (1898-1905). Some title deeds, which have emerged recently, indicate that Viscount Valentia bought some land at Stratton Audley Hall for £26 in 1872 and built kennels there. He was master then and presumably rebuilt or added to Drake's kennels. Both he and Lord Chesham served on the Imperial Yeomanry Committee when it was set up at the start of the Boer War in 1899, Viscount Valentia of Bletchington Park, Kirtlington, from the Oxford Yeomanry and Lord Chesham, from Twyford, Bucks, in command of the Royal Bucks Hussars. Their horsemanship was obviously invaluable. Lord Chesham died from a fall out hunting near Daventry in November 1907 and there is a plaque to him in Stratton Audley church.

The 1891 census shows John Brabazon as a visitor at the Hall, with no less than ten grooms and a stud groom. No doubt he was a guest of Lord Chesham or renting it himself for the hunting season. He was a colonel in the army and aide de camp to the Queen, which shows the high level of interest in the local hunting. He may well have been the father of Lord Brabazon of Tara (1884-1964), the noted aviator and politician, and Minister of Transport and then Aircraft Production during the Second World War.

Kenelm Charles Pepys, the 4th Earl of Cottenham, was master from 1895 to 1899, and at 21 he was the youngest master in England. His hunting box was at Bicester Hall on the corner of the London and

Launton roads. He was succeeded by Major (later Colonel) John Heywood-Lonsdale, DSO (1899-1922), who was away on active service during the 1914-18 War. His wife and Henry Tubb kept the Hunt going during this difficult time, when horses were being called-up for the war. In the first week of August 1914, at the start of the war, Britain's little army called up 165,000 horses, mounts for the cavalry and draught animals for the artillery and regimental transport waggons.[6112] Each division needed at least 5,000 horses. There was a huge loss of horses as the war progressed, and by 1917 fox hunting was almost dead.

The following succeeded Major Heywood-Lonsdale as master:

1922-25 The 5th Lord Chesham, until he was killed out hunting like his father.

1925-31 H.M.Budgett of Kirtlington. In this period and later, the Prince of Wales, later King Edward VIII, regularly rode with the Hunt

1931-33 Colonel John and his nephew, Captain Arthur Heywood-Lonsdale were joint masters. The Colonel built Poundon House, a few miles east of Stratton Audley.

1933-36 A committee managed the Hunt.

1936-42 Major R.E.Field-Marsham, who lived at Cotmore House after the War.

1937-39 Brig-Gen. A.Courage, DSO, MC.

1939-42 Colonel R.V.Buxton, DSO.

1942-45 The Hunt was managed by a committee, of which John Dewar-Harrison of Willaston, and Mrs Lloyd-Mostyn of Hethe, were key members.

1948-54 Mrs Loyd-Mostyn was joint master with P.J.Whiteley and then A.L.Beloe.

1954-63 A triumvirate of joint masters: R.A.Budgett, Capt H.M.Gosling and W.L.Pilkington. Capt Miles Gosling (1928-97), grandson of Col George Gosling of Stratton Audley Park, was also an amateur jockey, chairman of Cheltenham Racecourse between 1977 and 1990, and owner of racehorses in the 1960s.

1964- R.C.Smith Bingham and R. Cooper.

As the Hunt's Official Handbook of 1955 recorded: 'The Second World War was the most difficult period in the history of the Hunt, and its wonderful recovery after the War years was due in no small measure to her [Mrs Lloyd-Mostyn] devotion and generosity.' After the war, the area was divided into the Bicester South country and the Warden Hill country until 1948, with separate masters. The whole country was then

Mrs Margaret Lloyd-Mostyn in her pony and trap, which she used for visiting farmers to organise food for the Bicester hounds during the Second World War. (Sheila Johnson)

hunted by the Bicester & Warden Hill, until the amalgamation with the Whaddon Chase in 1985. The period covering 1923 to 1989 saw only three huntsmen, Clarence Johnson (1923-47) and his son Charlie (1947-64), and Brian Pheasey (1964-89). At the start of the Second World War, there was a similar call-up of horses by the Yeomanry. Charlie Johnson joined the Cheshire Yeomanry and they all collected horses before they sailed for Palestine. He wanted a particular horse, which he was able to identify out of hundreds, in spite of everyone's scepticism! Since 1989 Martin Thornton and now Patrick Martin have been the huntsmen.[6213]

The Whaddon Chase country was hunted under the mastership of the Selby Lowndes family from before 1750 until 1920. It was originally part of the country hunted by the Grafton family. The Hunt had its own masters until the commencement of the 1986-87 season, when it amalgamated with the Bicester & Warden Hill, as The Bicester Hunt with Whaddon Chase. On 1 May 2003, they were incorporated into a limited company, known as Bicester and Whaddon Chase Limited. Stratton Audley has continued as the centre of the Hunt to the present day. In spite of the anti-hunting legislation, support has remained very strong and in May 2008 new kennels were opened on the same site. From c.1930 until recently,

Charlie Johnson (Huntsman) and Mrs Marjorie Lloyd-Mostyn (Master) with the Bicester hounds at Quainton, early 1950s. (Sheila Johnson)

The Old Forge, Fringford, with Frederick Plumb (Matthew) in the cart c.1898. The smartly dressed boys were two of Kesia Whitton's nephews on a visit from Liverpool. (Bill Plumb)

the Boxing Day Meet in the Market Square was an outstanding event in the Bicester calendar. However, the prohibitive costs of policing the event have forced a move to Winslow. Apart from the hunting itself, the Hunt is involved in the popular local Point-to-Points and actively encourages the involvement of the young in the local Pony Clubs.

Hunt employment[14]

Since the early nineteenth century, a number of trades have been almost entirely dependent on the work provided by the Hunt. For many years these included saddlers, harness-makers, farriers, horseclippers, breeches-makers, sporting tailors, ostlers and grooms. So much was hand-made that Bicester and Brackley benefited enormously from the hunt trade. An early guide of the Automobile Association even referred to Bicester as a 'Horsey Little Town'. In the period prior to the outbreak of the 1914-18 War, the town in the winter was full of hunters, with stables in all parts of the town, including Kelly's Livery Stables off the Banbury Road (on the site of the present Stable Road). So many horses meant that three shoeing forges, three saddleries, and two coach-builders were very busy industries indeed, employing about fifty men.

Examination of the various trade directories for Bicester from 1876 to 1967 confirms the town's continuing involvement with the hunt trade, although it is noticeable that by 1924 there were many fewer listings. We must also remember that not everyone was listed in the directories and a full examination of the censuses might reveal others involved in the hunt trade. The three shoeing forges were Hugh Jagger, the vet, at 17 Market Square, Sirett and Waine at 25 Market Square and George Weston Sirett at 7 Causeway. Walter Haynes, assisted by two of his sons, also set up as a blacksmith in 1912 at 29 Causeway. He was succeeded by his widow, Mrs Kate Haynes, but the business terminated in 1939, when there were still two other smiths, Tom Allan Almond at 1 Causeway and H.Hazell & Son at 21 Market Square. By 1967, John N.Almond was at the same address but as a sports outfitter.

The three saddle and harness makers were William Davey (later Almonds) at 1 Causeway, John Stuchfield at 24 Market Square and Mrs Agnes Tompkins at 15 Sheep Street. John Stuchfield, junior, was still in business at 24 Market Square in 1924. By 1939 A.A.Tompkins had a new proprietor, F.R. Brown. The wheelwrights/coach-builders were William Parrott in Kings End and William Townsend, who ran a business founded in 1810 in Church Street. The Townsends sold the business to Jack Hollis in 1923 and he remained in business until the War. There were a few saddlers in the villages outside Bicester but many villages had a blacksmith or two, at least until the 1950s. In the Shelswell Group, Fringford, Stoke Lyne and Stratton Audley still had blacksmiths listed in 1939, and in Fringford Jackman and Perrin continued working into the 1950s.

The figures below for Stratton Audley in the late nineteenth century confirm the high numbers dependent on the Hunt. The 1861 census for Stratton records a gentleman's coachman, four grooms/stablemen, a colt breaker, two blacksmiths and a kennel man, nine in all. By 1871 there were at least eight grooms, a stud groom, a huntsman, a first and second whip, three coachmen and a second horseman, 16 in all. In 1881 there was a kennel man/huntsman, a huntsman, two stud grooms/huntsmen, 18 grooms/stablemen, a coachman, a horsetrainer, two blacksmiths, and two whippers-in/huntsmen, 28 in total. The blacksmiths or farriers were crucial to the hunting stables, as we can see in *Lark Rise to Candleford*: 'three times a week, Matthew and two of the shoeing smiths drove off with strings of horseshoes and boxes of tools to visit the hunting stables.'[15] Matthew is based on Frederick Plumb, who was working at Fringford forge when Flora was there in the 1890s.

Flora also gives a colourful description of the annual meet of the Bicester Hunt on the first Saturday in January, which met at the Butchers Arms in Fringford. 'The whole neighbourhood turned out to see the Meet.

Col. George Gosling of Stratton Audley Park with his farm bailiff, William Norton, 1914. (Anne Townsend)

Both roadways were lined with little low basketwork pony-carriages with elderly ladies in furs, governess-cars with nurses and children, farm carts with forks stuck upright in loads of manure, and butcher's carts and grocer's carts and baker's white-tilted vans, and donkey-barrows in which red-faced, hoarse-shouting hawkers stood up for a better view. Matthew used to say that it was a funny thing that everybody's errand led them in that direction on Meet Morning.' Matthew himself set a fine example: 'Every year, as soon as the Meet was assembled, Matthew would hang up his apron, slip into his second-best coat, and say that he must just pop across the green for a moment; Squire, or Sir Austin, or Muster Ramsbottom of Pilvery had asked him to run his hand over his mare's fetlock.'[16]

By 1891 Stratton Audley Park, which had been built by George Glen (d.1885) in 1860, Stratton Audley Hall and the Manor House all had a complement of hunting staff. George Gosling was living at the Park, John Blundell-Leigh at the Manor House, and John Brabazon was a visitor at the Hall. It is difficult to be sure who employed whom; however, Brabazon certainly had 10 grooms and a stud groom, while Gosling had at least two coachmen, three stablemen/grooms, and a stud groom. Others dependent on the hunt included a coachman/groom, 18 grooms, a stud groom, two kennel men, a second horseman, a huntsman, a first whip, and a blacksmith. The total of 43 was a significant number in a village population of 405. The 1901 census shows a similar pattern of employment. There were three grooms at the Manor, at least 13 at the Hunt (Livery) Stables, four at Stratton Audley Hall with John B. Kingscote, and 9 at Stratton Audley Park with Colonel Gosling. Others dependent on the hunt included a huntsman, a first whipper-in, a gamekeeper, a blacksmith, and a coachman. The blacksmith was Joseph Phillips, who was still working there in 1939. The total of 34 was again a significant number in a village population of 336.

The above figures, of course, do not include other followers of the Hunt, either living locally or visiting for the hunting season, who would also have provided employment and business for the local area. In 1901, for example, Edward Slater-Harrison (Sir Timothy) had three grooms at Shelswell Park and Sir Algernon Peyton five grooms at Swift's House. As a further indication of the support for the Hunt in this period, some hundred hunters used to be stabled in Bicester during the hunting season (November to end-March). In spite of problems during the First World War, support for the Hunt continued. After the war, Stratton Audley was dominated by Mrs Smyly at the Hall, Mrs Beckwith-Smith at the Manor and Mrs Gosling at the Park, who were all active supporters of the Hunt. Mrs Smyly was one of the Rigden brewing family, who had moved from Kent to Stratton Audley in the 1920s. In addition to the Manor, Mrs Smyly also bought Fringford Lodge from Frederick Withington, as a hunting box. Betty Rigden, her niece, lived and farmed there and she also became a well-known breeder of horses, as we shall see below.

Special trains[17]

By the late nineteenth century, there were special hunting season tickets for horses and grooms on the Great Western Railway (GWR). In more recent times, there were still regular special trains locally for the Hunt. One of these ran from Bicester and another from Finmere, until the station closed in 1966. You can still see the old stables behind the Shelswell Arms, across from the old Finmere station. The special trains included a van for the hounds, a coach for the huntsmen, and another one for the hunt subscribers. The trains used to take them all to Woodford Halse for good hunting country further north. There could be 300 riders involved, many of them with second horses to be ridden when the first ones were exhausted. Even today the master and key riders will have second horses. On their return to Finmere, there was a tray of drinks ready, to be drunk

GWR advertisement for the Hunting Season, with special tickets for grooms and horses, 1903.

quickly, as the hounds were stiff and needed to be on their way back to the kennels in Stratton Audley.

The GWR service timetables used to carry a warning about hunting country 'Every care must be taken to avoid running over Packs of Hounds, which, during the Hunting Season, may cross them.' Locally, whenever the Bicester hounds were hunting near a railway line, the earth-stoppers used to run up the track before a train came and set deto-nators. These would be triggered by the oncoming train and warn the driver to slow down. The number of the engine would be noted and a collection made for the driver and delivered to him that evening – so much for old style courtesy! The earth-stoppers were generally farmhand volunteers from the area, and there is still an annual thank-you dinner for all of them. There was more than local interest in the Bicester Hunt, so the National Press used to ring the local post office daily to get news of the day's hunting.

I hope that this has shown the considerable impact of hunting on this area for well over two hundred years. The Bicester Hunt still has 49 couples of hounds, and receives tremendous support, while the kennels continue to provide employment. Hunting is surely an important part of our heritage and not one to be destroyed lightly at the whim of any government. It has provided and, in spite of any anti-hunting legislation, is likely to continue to provide enormous pleasure to young and old and employment to many. Those involved show great respect and under-standing of the countryside and country pursuits. This must surely be of great value, particularly as new building encroaches ever more quickly into our green spaces. Current plans for the expansion of Bicester are just one example of this encroachment.

The Turf

There is a remarkable link between a local man and the Grand National. Frederick Withington (1869-1951) was the son of the Revd Edward Withington, who lived at Fringford Lodge on the Bicester road. After his education at Eton, he became a leading amateur jockey. On giving up riding in 1899, he trained steeplechase horses at Danebury, near Stockbridge, Hants. In about 1920 he moved back to Oxfordshire, first to Lodge Farm, Fritwell and then to the family home at Fringford Lodge. His major success came in 1908, when he had the first two home in the Grand National, the only time that this has been achieved.

The story of Rubio's victory in the 1908 Grand National is a romantic one. He won three races in 1903 but broke down badly. An extraordinary decision was then taken to send him to the landlord of the Prospect Arms in Towcester, where he would pull an omnibus in a harness in order to ferry guests between the station and the hotel. This was so successful that he was back in training in 1906. In 1908 he was entered for the Grand National but as the second string in the stable to the favourite, Mattie Macgregor. In the event he won by ten lengths from Mattie Macgregor, the only time that the first two horses have come from the same stable.

In the 1920s Vivian Hugh-Smith, subsequently created Baron Bicester of Tusmore in 1938, and Col E.H.Wyndham of Caversfield House, Bicester, both became patrons of Fred Withington. The Colonel owned a horse called Red Splash, which Fred trained to win the first running of the Cheltenham Gold Cup in 1924. The Fred Withington Chase was run in his memory for many years at Cheltenham. It was in the post-war years that Lord Bicester, who was chairman of the Bicester Hunt Committee, enjoyed his greatest success with horses like Three Chestnuts, Silver Fame, Roimond and Finnure. In 1952 Silver Fame won the Cheltenham Gold Cup and overall won ten races there, an all-time record. Although Lord Bicester never won the Grand National, in 1949 Roimond came a close second to Russian Hero.

Other local connections with the Turf have included Betty Rigden of Fringford Lodge, who was a well-known breeder. She was part-owner of Windmill Girl, who was mother to two Derby winners: Blakeney (1969) and Morston (1973). Both were trained by Arthur Budgett of Kirtlington. More recently, Paddy McMahon of Fringford achieved fame in the equestrian world with his great horse, Penward Forge Mill.

Notes

1   J.C. Blomfield, *Deanery of Bicester*, Part VII, 85 (1893).

2   Blomfield, *Deanery of* Bicester, Part III, 23.

3   W.J. Reader, *At Duty's Call, A Study in Obsolete Patriotism*, 33.

4   Christine Bloxham, *The World of Flora Thompson Revisited*, 61-3.

5   John Betjeman, *Betjeman's Britain*, 185.

6   For this section I am indebted to Ralph Greaves, *A Short History of the Bicester & Warden Hill Hunt*, and to Sheila Johnson and Albert Parker.

7   The Rotary Club of Bicester, *The Bicester Story*, 147.

8   John M. Sergeant, *A History of Fringford and Newton-cum-Shelswell*.

9   Blomfield, *Deanery of Bicester*, Part III, 38, and Peter Bushell, *Swift's House, Stoke Lyne, A History*, for the quotation from *The Times*.

10 Blomfield, *Deanery of Bicester*, Part VIII, 23-25.

11 Blomfield, *Deanery of Bicester*, Part VIII, 27.

12 John Keegan, *The First World War*, 83.

13 For this section I am indebted to *The Bicester Story*, 147-8, and to Sheila Johnson. and Albert Parker.

14 For this section I am indebted to David Watts and Peter Barrington's *The Changing Faces of Bicester,* Part V, Section Four, 74-80.

15 Flora Thompson, *Lark Rise to Candleford*, 370.

16 Thompson, *Lark Rise*, 420.

17 For this section I am much indebted to Sheila Johnson.

Chapter 5

Schools and Education

'What do our young Alf want wi' a lot o' book larnin'?' they would say.
'He can read and write and add up as much money as he's ever
likely to get. What more do he want?'[1]

When Flora was growing up in the 1880s, a section of the people still
resented their boys being kept at school when they might be
earning. They could join their fathers on the land, aged eight or less, and
make a useful contribution to the family budget. However, Forster's
Education Act of 1870 provided that elementary schools should be established wherever school provision was insufficient. This was followed by
further legislation in 1876 and 1880, which established that all children
should receive elementary education and that school attendance to the age
of ten was compulsory. Before we look at the effect of all this legislation,
let us examine what schools and education had been available before.

Early schools

Before the early nineteenth century, there was very little if any education for the children in most of the Shelswell villages. Finmere and
Fringford seem to have been the exceptions. In Finmere there was a small
school as early as 1739, and by 1779 a school for some seventy children
under the first recorded teacher, William Malins. This seems a large
number for a parish of some three hundred people but Malins had ten children himself! In Fringford there was a similar small school by 1768,
teaching the catechism, reading and writing. In the early nineteenth
century, both villages were particularly fortunate in the wealth and
support of their rectors, Willam Palmer and Henry Roundell, who both
dominated their communities from 1814 to 1852.

In 1824 Palmer, with the aid of the Duke of Buckingham, had a new
school built in Finmere 'for the use and benefit of the poor children of the
parish, under the direction of the Church and its ministers.' He also had

Laura (Olivia Hallinan) in the BBC television series, 2008 (BBC Photo Library)

plate ii   In Flora's Footsteps

Twister (Karl Johnson) and Queenie (Linda Bassett) in the BBC television series, 2008 (BBC Photo Library)

Dorcas Lane (Julia Sawalha) and Sir Timothy (Ben Miles) in the BBC television series, 2008 (BBC Photo Library)

plate iv   In Flora's Footsteps

The cast-iron cross marking the grave of Zilpha Hinks (Zillah), who died in 1900 aged 45. There are more crosses of this type in Fringford churchyard (24) than anywhere else in Oxfordshire (Peter Silver)

Fringford Old Rectory, the impressive home of Revd Coker (Mr Coulsdon) and his successor, Revd Thompson (Mr Delafield) (Jinkie Hebditch/the author)

plate vi   *In Flora's Footsteps*

Stratton Audley

Hardwick

Hethe

Newton Purcell

Fringford

Above and opposite: Collage of the ten Shelswell Churches, painted as a leaving present for the Revd Ricky Yates, 31 August 2008 (Julie Barrett)

Mixbury

Stoke Lyne

Godington

Cottisford

Finmere

plate viii   *In Flora's Footsteps*

Shelswell Park stable block after its restoration in 2000 (Baroness von Maltzahn)

Tusmore Park, 2005 (Wafic Said and June Buck / Country Life Picture Library)

plate x   *In Flora's Footsteps*

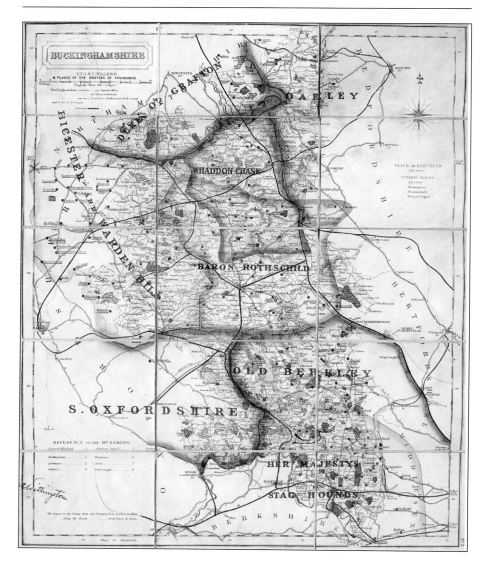

J. & C. Walker's Fox Hunting Map of Buckinghamshire, 1830s (Sheila Johnson)

Above: Fringford Old School, 2007, now converted to a private house. (Julie Barrett)

Below: Newton Purcell School, 1971. Note the datestones, 1873 for the original building on the right, and 1899 for the enlargement on the left. It closed in 1957. (OCC)

plate xii   In Flora's Footsteps

Above: Thatched cottages, Main Street, Fringford, 2007. Lizzie Grantham's sweet shop was in the cottage to the right of the thatched ones. (Julie Barrett)

Below: Old Bake House, Fringford, 2007. Les Morgan was the last man to run the bakery, in the late 1960s. (Julie Barrett)

'Dew's Groceries, Haberdashery and Ironmongery Store', Fritwell. It was built by Frank Dew in 1885 and it was said to have been the largest village store in England. It closed in the 1970s and has been converted into luxury apartments. (The author)

plate xiv   In Flora's Footsteps

Above and opposite: Both sides of the Banner of the Mansfield Lodge of the Independent Order of the Oddfellows (Manchester Unity) No.3904. (Fringford Village Hall)

plate xvi   In Flora's Footsteps

'Motor House 1902', Tusmore Park, the charming name for one of the first private garages in England. (The author)

Cottisford School, where Flora went to school in the 1880s, 1905. (OCC)

a new school built in Mixbury in 1838. In Fringford Roundell ensured that daily and Sunday schools were always available for boys and girls. It was his successor, Henry de Salis, who built the National School in 1866 on land leased from the squire, John Slater-Harrison. By the early nineteenth century, most of the other villages had some form of education, mainly dame schools and Sunday schools. However, many of these were short-lived and even in 1838 Roundell commented that 'six places have no daily or Sunday school'.

Education Acts

There was a spate of school building between 1852 and 1873, thanks to the efforts of the incumbents and the local squires (Table 6). Shortly after this, legislation of 1876 required all children aged five to ten to attend school. Older children were obliged to attend for a minimum of 250 half-days until they were twelve and for 150 days until they were fourteen. They could only leave earlier if they passed the 'labour certificate' – an examination in the three Rs. However, attendance was sporadic in many rural schools, as there were many distractions. Young boys left early to work on the farms and young girls to do lacemaking and sewing. Attendance did improve but the Attendance Officer remained a regular feature of school life until the end of the nineteenth century.

Cottisford (Fordlow) school, together with a two-roomed cottage for the schoolmistress, was built in 1856 by the Revd Charles Harrison (Mr Ellison).

Table 6   Shelswell Schools 1824-2008

Parish	Built	-----Reorganised-----			Closed	
Cottisford CE	1856				1968	Note 1
Finmere CE	1824	1926			1948	Note 2
Finmere CE	1959					Note 3
Fringford CE	1866	1929/31	1949	1951	1973	Note 4
Fringford CE	1973	2003				Note 5
Hardwick	1870				c.1900	Note 6
Hethe CE	1852	1924	1948		1973	Note 7
Hethe Catholic	1870	1920			1930	Note 8
Mixbury CE	1838	1928	1948	1954	1955	Note 9
Newton Purcell CE	1873	1929	1952		1957	Note 10
Stoke Lyne CE	1864	1930			1985	Note 11
Stratton Audley CE	1837	1929	1951		1973	Note 12

Notes

1. Cottisford closed from 1920 to 1924, when it became a Council school.

2. Finmere senior pupils were sent to Fringford in 1926. When the school closed in 1948, infants were sent to Mixbury and juniors to Fringford.

3. In 1959 a new school was opened in Finmere with 46 on roll.

4. In 1929 a fourth classroom was added to Fringford, allowing admission of children over 11 from Cottisford, Hethe, Newton Purcell and Stratton Audley. In 1931 a fifth classroom ('the Hut') was erected at a cost of £125. In 1949 Fringford was reorganised as a Junior Central School, with ages 5-7 coming from Fringford and Godington, and ages 8-11 from Fringford, Hardwick, Hethe, Godington, Cotmore and Caversfield. Seniors now moved on to Bicester. In 1951 the managers handed the school over to the LEA.

5. In 1973 the Old School in Fringford closed and the children moved into the new school. In 2003 the Shelswell Playgroup moved to the new school site.

6. Hardwick school was built by the Earl of Effingham but was never recognised as a public elementary school. It closed c.1895-1903.

7. Hethe senior pupils were sent to Fringford in 1924. In 1948 children aged 8-11 were were sent to Fringford and seniors moved on to Bicester. The school closed in 1973.

8. By 1920 Hethe RC school was infants only and it closed in 1930. It reopened from 1940 to 1943 to accommodate up to 60 evacuees from London.

9. In 1928 Mixbury school was reorganised as a junior school and seniors were sent to Fringford. In 1948 it was reorganised as an infants' school. In 1954 it was granted aided status but it closed in 1955.

10. In 1929 children over 11 from Newton Purcell were sent to Fringford. In 1952 the school was granted aided status but it closed in 1957. Children went to Fringford for one year and then to the new Finmere school.

11. In 1930 Stoke Lyne was reorganised as a junior school and seniors were sent to Fritwell. In 1985 the school closed and pupils were all transferred to Fritwell.

12. In 1929 children over 11 from Stratton Audley were sent to Fringford. In 1951 it became a controlled school under the LEA. It closed in 1973.

Fringford May Queen, Jean Faulkner, in the early 1950s, with the Revd Westlake and Len Standen, the headmaster, in the back row. (Judy Legg)

'Reading, writing, and arithmetic were the principal subjects, with a Scripture lesson every morning, and needlework every afternoon for the girls. There was no assistant mistress; Governess [Miss Holmes] taught all the classes simultaneously, assisted only by two monitors – ex-scholars, aged about twelve, who were paid a shilling a week each for their services.'[2] It must have been a hard task for Miss Holmes, who did carry a cane about with her. She seldom used it on the girls and still more seldom on the infants, although it served with the boys. 'It must be remembered that in those days a boy of eleven was nearing the end of his school life. Soon he would be at work; already he felt himself nearly a man and too old for petticoat government.'[3]

These were changing times, and the position of a village schoolmistress, like Miss Holmes, was a trying one socially. As Flora wrote later, 'Perhaps it is still trying in some places, for it is not many years ago that the President of a Women's Institute wrote: "We are very democratic here. Our Committee consists of three ladies, three women, and the village schoolmistress." That mistress, though neither lady nor woman, was still placed. In the 'eighties the schoolmistress was so nearly a new institution that a vicar's wife, in a real dilemma said: "I should like to ask Miss So and So to tea; but do I ask her to kitchen or dining-room tea?"'[4]

Fringford Old School, built in 1866, 1920s. It closed in 1973. (OCC)

The greatest day in the year from the children's point of view was May Day. Flora gives a very detailed and possibly embroidered description of the celebrations, which were organised by the school. The children, with the Queen and the garland, visited Cottisford House and the rest of the houses in the village. They then carried on beyond the parish boundary on a seven-mile circuit, which would have included Shelswell House. Things did not all go smoothly. Feet got tired, there were squabbles among the boys, 'or some irate gamekeeper would turn the procession back from a short cut, adding miles to the way. But these were slight drawbacks to happiness on a day as near to perfection as anything can be in human life.'[5] Similar celebrations carried on at least into the 1950s.

The twentieth century

In 1902 the local authorities were given responsibility for elementary and secondary education. The leaving age was now twelve, except for children employed in agriculture. The Fringford logbooks show that harvests continued to be a considerable distraction, particularly during both World Wars. Gardening was added to the curriculum in 1914 and the subject was taken seriously with the need for extra food during wartime. The rector provided a plot in the Bridge Ground Allotments near Fringford Bridge and in 1915 Arthur Jepson, the headmaster, passed the exam in Cottage and Allotment Gardening held by the Royal Horticultural Society.

A late harvest could delay the start of school, as it did in September 1917, when the children were granted an additional week's holiday. The potato harvest in September and October could have a similar effect, particularly in wartime, and there were school holidays of a week or more for the harvest during both World Wars. The children were also given a series of half-holidays to pick blackberries (to make jam) for the Army and Navy in 1917 and 1918. As a result, in July 1917 the Government had to announce that marks lost by children employed in harvests after the holidays would be allowed for.

Evacuees

During the Second World War, some three million children were evacuated from London, starting on 1 September 1939, just two days before the Declaration of War. Locally, there was a considerable impact on the schools and communities. On 1 September 800 children and teachers were evacuated from London to Bicester by train; 168 were billeted in the town, the remainder in villages in the Ploughley area. On 2 September 600 mothers and young children arrived from London; 150 were housed in Bicester, 450 in Ploughley villages.[6] In Finmere, the evacuees doubled the school roll. In Fringford, a party of 40 children from the William McGuffie School in Walthamstow arrived in June 1940, and this enlarged the school to five classes with 140 on the roll. The roll even reached 159 in October 1940, compared

Schoolchildren in front of Fringford school c.1910. (Sue Gahan)

Mrs. E. Hinks.

Certificate, signed by the Queen Mother, given to Mrs Emily Hinks of Fringford, for providing a home to evacuees in 1939-40. (Gladys Hinks)

to the pre-war 90. Cottisford too received its fair share of evacuees, most of whom were allocated in ones and twos to private households. However, 'Lady Brook-Popham established a 'War Nursery' at Cottisford House where several dozen young evacuees were accomodated.'[7]

Although the evacuees arrived with their own teachers, their arrival must have been a major disruption to the lives of the schools and the local residents. The Fringford logbook comments that the evacuees 'are constantly changing, some returning to their home towns and others being admitted, so that the classes are by no means settled'. The evacuee teachers also changed. One ex-pupil from that period told me that her parents took her away from Fringford and sent her to Oxford as 'she was learning nothing'! Things did not return to normal until September 1945, when the numbers on roll in Fringford were back down to 90.[8]

Hethe also experienced an influx of evacuees. In June 1940 St Philip's RC School re-opened especially to receive some 30 children from St Patrick's School, Walthamstow, under the escort of nuns. The numbers peaked to around 60 in 1941, when the schoolroom, now divided into two, would have been shockingly overcrowded by modern standards. By June 1943, however, only 17 children remained and the school closed for the last time. In addition to these evacuees, a convent school was evacuated from Norwood, the juniors to Fringford Manor and the seniors to Swift's House, Stoke Lyne. They had their lessons there but every Sunday both schools used to walk in crocodile to St Philip's church, the juniors in dark brown uniforms, the seniors in dark blue ones.[9]

The disruption for the schools and all the host families is obvious. What is much more difficult to assess is the effect on the evacuees, and this is really beyond the remit of this book. However, I might mention a couple of cases arising from my earlier research into the Fringford evacuees. They serve to show, like a recent BBC programme presented by Michael Aspel (himself an evacuee), how varied their experiences could be. In one instance, where a brother and sister were billeted separately, the brother had a very good time, while the sister was very poorly treated. He made good friends with another evacuee on one of the farms and spent much of his time playing happily there. By contrast, his sister's family, among other things, kept all the food parcels sent by her mother and ate the food themselves. In another case, a boy, who had been evacuated to Stratton Audley, explained to me a few years ago how he had been saved from a life of crime. He had been involved in a gang on the streets of Walthamstow before he was evacuated. His hostess was the formidable Mrs Smyly, who made sure that he behaved. After leaving school, he worked at Moat Farm, Godington, where he was so happy that initially he refused to return to his mother.

These few examples show how varied the experiences of the evacuees must have been. Surviving photographs show how devastating it was for these little children and for their parents. It was also a huge shock for these rural communities to receive urban children who were so different from their own. Many local people took a series of evacuees into their homes and treated them with great kindness. It was a nice touch that a certificate, signed by the Queen Mother, was sent to all those people who had given a home to evacuees for 28 weeks or more. There is much to be written still about the experiences of these evacuees, particularly with the seventieth anniversary due in September 2009.

School reorganisations

Over the years, there were a number of reorganisations of the schools, as set out in Table 6. I will only comment on the major ones. In 1929 a fourth classroom was added to Fringford school, which allowed the admission of older children (over 11) from Cottisford, Hethe, Newton Purcell and Stratton Audley. In 1931 a fifth classroom ('the Hut') was erected at a cost of £125, mainly for practical work. In 1946 the leaving age was raised to 15. In 1949 Fringford was reorganised as a Junior Central School, with ages 5-7 coming from Fringford and Godington, and ages 8-11 from Fringford, Hardwick, Hethe, Godington, Cotmore and

Stratton Audley School, built in 1837, 1905. It closed in 1973. (OCC)

Caversfield. Seniors now moved on to Bicester, where the new Highfield Secondary Modern School was built off Queen's Avenue in 1951. Stoke Lyne was the only school not involved in this reorganisation. In 1930 their school had been reorganised as a Junior School and seniors were sent to Fritwell. When the school closed in 1985, all the children were transferred to Fritwell, not to Fringford.

Our remaining schools

In September 1959 a new school was opened in Finmere. The new groundbreaking design was much admired and it had a notable influence on the design of village schools. 'The new school at Finmere set the whole trend of primary school design for the 1960s [providing] a greater measure of learning opportunity for fifty children than had ever been achieved before.'[10] The school was successful until the 1990s but in 1995 it was placed in 'special measures', following a critical report by OFSTED, and pupil numbers declined significantly. Since then numbers and teaching have improved, although the roll is still low and closure has been considered.

Fringford is now the only other village in the Benefice with a school. In 1973 Fringford 'old school' was closed and the 'new school' was opened on the other side of the Green. The 'old school' became a Victorian Study Centre and in the early 1980s 'the Hut' became home to the Shelswell Playgroup. In 2003, the Playgroup relocated to a new building on the 'new school' site. In 2004, the 'old school' site was sold and the school building was converted to a superior private house. Conversion included the demolition of 'the Hut', which had been erected in 1931 at a cost of £125! The 'new school', after some difficult times in the 1980s, continues to flourish with over 100 pupils on roll. To many people the site seems an obvious one for expansion but the Local Education Authority has so far resisted all requests for an extra classroom.

Notes

1   Flora Thompson, *Lark Rise to Candleford*, 182.
2   Thompson, *Lark Rise*, 178-9.
3   Thompson, *Lark Rise*, 182.
4   Thompson, *Lark Rise*, 196.
5   Thompson, *Lark Rise*, 201-8, and Christine Bloxham, *The World of Flora Thompson Revisited*, 82-4.
6   Bicester Guide & Directory 1953.
7   Ted & Joan Flaxman, *Cottisford Revisited*, 52.
8   M.W. Greenwood, *Fringford Through the Ages*, 49.
9   Joy Grant, *Hethe-with-Adderbury, The Story of a Catholic Parish in Oxfordshire*, 79.
10   Finmere and Little Tingewick Historical Society, *The Millennium History of Finmere*, 73-6.

Chapter 6

Changes in Village Life

'Every member of the community knew his or her place
and few wished to change it.'[1]

Flora describes a very ordered community, in which 'those at the top had no reason to wish for change and by others the social order was so generally accepted that there was no sense of injustice.' In historian's terms, all the Shelswell villages were 'closed' rather than 'open'. A closed village may be described as one where a squire or absentee landlord owns at least half the acreage, while an open village would have many small proprietors. The control of the local squires was often enhanced by the local rector's holdings of glebe land. In the Shelswell villages, the only possible exceptions to this control were in Hethe, where the strong Methodist congregation provided a dissenting element, and in Juniper Hill, as we have seen, by the likes of Albert Timms and the Ranters. In the previous chapters we have examined some of the major influences on the life of those living in these villages. In this chapter, I look at some of the more general changes in village life since Flora's Victorian childhood.

Population

The Shelswell Group population figures from 1801 to 2001 (Table 7) show clearly how the village populations declined between 1871 and 1901, down from 3,129 to 2,249 in total. In this period the rural population of Oxfordshire declined from 101,517 to 92,859. At the same time the population of Oxford increased from 34,482 to 49,285, and the population of England and Wales by some 43% to 32,528,000. The figures for individual Shelswell villages in the nineteenth century show that most of them had their peak populations between 1851 and 1871 and the others before 1851.

The agricultural depression of 1874-84 brought an end to the farming boom of the 1860s, and caused severe rural poverty. This was aggravated by a second agricultural depression from 1891-99, partly caused by foreign competition, with frozen meat coming in from Australia, New Zealand and South America. Even in Lark Rise 'The Innkeeper's wife got in cases of tinned salmon and Australian rabbit.'[2] There was also growing competition from mass-produced goods and declining local markets, which affected, for example, bootmakers, blacksmiths, tailors and wheel-wrights. It also affected women's employment, as we shall see below.

These depressions contributed to large numbers moving to the towns or emigrating. Between 1871 and 1911 six million Britons emigrated, with the peak in the 1870s and 1890s. Most of them were men from rural areas, so that by 1900 there were over one million more women than men in Britain. Advertisements in the *Bicester Advertiser* at the time included many offers of free land, in Canada, New Zealand and Australia. By 1901, however, Canada was 'the only country offering free land to home seekers of limited means.' No less than 50,000 per annum were entering her ports. In many cases the parishes also gave some support to those wishing to emigrate, as they had done earlier in the nineteenth century. In addition, by the late 1890s men in the villages with any ambition were looking for wider opportunities in factories, on the railways and docks, and in the new urban police forces.

In the twentieth century, there was further decline in the Shelswell populations at least until 1951, when the total was only 2,020 compared to 2,249 in 1901. Even in 2001 the total was only 2,560. Most of this increase was in Finmere and Fringford, where there were new housing developments in the 1960s and 1980s.

Agriculture

We saw above how poor and largely dependent on agriculture the people in Lark Rise were. Their lives were simple but hard, with few luxuries. This would also have been true of the other villages in the Shelswell Group. In Fringford, for example, in 1851 there were 61 labourers out of a population of 357 and there were similar numbers in 1891, when the population was 403 and the youngest recorded labourer was only eleven. If you include all those employed in occupations related to agriculture, for example, carters, hurdle makers, shepherds and wheelwrights, there were 73 in 1851 rising to 93 in 1891. These totals represent 50% rising to 59% of all males over ten in the village. Given the agricultural depressions in the 1870s and 1880s, these figures seem high and it is likely that some of these labourers may not have been fully employed by 1891. By 1901, when the population had fallen to 335, there were only 35 labourers.

Table 7
Population in the Shelswell Group 1801-2001

Village	1801	1851	1871	1901	1931	1951	2001
Cottisford (Note 1)	106	263	**269**	175	139	154	156
Finmere	308	**399**	327	226	187	265	436
Fringford	252	357	**479**	335	268	331	613
Godington	99	87	70	57	60	45	40
Hardwick (Note 2)	61	66	74	46	37	113	53
Tusmore(Note 2)	31	**52**	43	51	82		
Hethe	262	418	393	311	293	288	279
Mixbury	304	**402**	338	221	186	184	255
Newton Purcell	93	117	122	103	130	103	103
Shelswell (Note 3)	42	43	43	45			
Stoke Lyne (Note 4)	334	**631**	603	409	381	231	232
Stratton Audley	**379**	305	368	270	327	306	393
Total	2,271	3,140	3,129	2,249	2,090	2,020	2,560

Town

	1801	1851	1871	1901	1931	1951	2001
Banbury	3,810	8,206	9,863	**10,012**	13,998	18,916	41,802
Bicester	1,946	3,054	3,328	3,023	3,110	4,171	28,672
Brackley	1,515	2,277	2,331	2,487	2,097	2,531	13,331
Chipping Norton	2,200	3,368	4,092	4,130	3,499	3,878	5,972
Oxford	12,604	26,773	34,482	**49,285**	80,539	98,684	134,248
Oxfordshire(Note 5)	111,977	170,434	177,960	181,149	209,784	275,808	605,488

Bold type = peak population 1801-1901

Other dates for peak populations 1801-1901:

1821 Hardwick 98	1861 Hethe 442
1821 Newton Purcell 143	1881 Chipping Norton 4,607
1821 Shelswell 51	1891 Bicester 3,343
1831 Godington 118	1891 Brackley 2,614

Notes

1. Cottisford includes Juniper Hill.

2. Hardwick and Tusmore were combined as a civil parish in 1932.

3. Shelswell was combined with Newton Purcell from 1911.

4. In 1948 Fewcott was transferred from Stoke Lyne to Ardley parish.

5. The large increase in the population of Oxfordshire by 2001 is partly due to the incorporation of part of Berkshire in 1974.

The Wyatt family with horses and a Trapper mowing machine, Manor Farm, Hethe c.1910. In the left-hand corner you can just see the milk cans, which the elegant Mary would have brought for the thirsty family. (OCC)

There were seven active farms in Fringford in 1851, farming from 50 to over 500 acres, and there were still six in 1939 (Table 8). The big difference between the two dates is that, with the growth of mechanisation, the farms were no longer so labour intensive by 1939. Trade directories indicate that the number of farms in the other parishes also remained relatively constant over the same period. It has to be borne in mind that the information in the directories is only as accurate as the source, generally the parish clerk. In Finmere there are seven farms recorded in 1852 and five in 1939, in Mixbury, five and six respectively, in Stoke Lyne, seven and six, and in Stratton Audley, nine and seven.

It is also interesting to look at the number of mills which have operated in the Shelswell Group. Their story goes back at least to Domesday in 1086, when two mills were recorded at Fringford, one at Godington and two at Mixbury. Fringford Mill, which was operated for over thirty years by Thomas Hanks Allen, continued to grind corn until 1947. The local farmers also used to bring their sheep for washing in the mill-stream (not for dipping with chemicals). The only other mill which operated in recent times was at Oldfields Farm, Stratton Audley and this ceased milling in the 1930s.

In 1943 the Banburyshire region, just to the north of the Shelswell Group, was chosen out of all England for a systematic study and film of

Thomas Hanks Allen, of Fringford Mill, threshing at Waterloo Farm, Fringford, 1920s. (Thomas Henry Allen)

rural life under the title 'Twenty-Four Square Miles'. The chosen area included Banbury and was bounded on the west by Hook Norton and the Sibfords, and on the south by Deddington. The film and report highlighted the extent of the decline in agriculture since the depressions of the late nineteenth century and the poor state of rural housing. It revealed that less than one-third of the working population was then working on the land. It also showed the dire need for post-war reconstruction. In most of the villages surveyed, electricity and mains water did not arrive until the late 1950s or early 1960s, nor new housing until around the same time. The findings in the Shelswell villages at the time would no doubt have been very similar.

Today all the Shelswell parishes remain agricultural but nationwide less than 2% of the working population now work on the land. A recent article illustrated just how much mechanisation has changed the face of farming.[3] In the 1930s, a farmer using a single furrow plough with a horse could plough an acre a day, so doing his 30-acre field would take the whole of January. After the war, when he got his first tractor, he could pull a five-furrow plough, which meant he could do his 30-acre field in just over a day. Later, contractors with 10-furrow ploughs could do the field by dinner

Fringford Mill, sheep washing, 1920s. The water mill was used for corn grinding until 1947. (Thomas Henry Allen)

time. Today, with the new monster machines, the ploughing record is 321 hectares (about 800 acres) in 24 hours. The number of farms has declined significantly as their acreage has increased and in Fringford, for example,

Fringford Mill, cleaning party, c.1920. This was a casual group hired to clean the mill-stream. (Thomas Henry Allen)

the only large-scale farmer is David Taylor at Waterloo Farm. In sharp contrast to his father and grandfather, he farms some 1800 acres with just two helpers and some very large machinery. There must have been a similar change in the other parishes.

Wages

As we have seen, life was hard in Lark Rise and elsewhere, particularly for the labourers, whose wages were only some ten shillings per week. It has been said that 'low wages provided an existence not a life'. However, 'After the Jubilee [the Golden Jubilee of 1887], nothing ever seemed quite the same.' A change of farmers saw the introduction of 'the new self-binding reaping machine and women were no longer required in the harvest field.' 'Wages rose, prices soared, and new needs multiplied.' 'Then, about that time, came a rise in wages. Agricultural workers were given fifteen instead of ten or twelve shillings a week, and skilled craftsmen were paid an agreed rate per hour, instead of the former weekly wage, irrespective of the time put in.'[4]

The provision of allotments in many villages during the nineteenth century was also a significant benefit for the poor, allowing them to live off their own produce. In Fringford, for example, the Revd Henry Roundell (1814-52) 'commenced the plan of letting small allotments of land to the labourers of the parish, devoting some glebe to that purpose, a rare kindness at that time [1830s].'[15] In Juniper Hill eight acres of allot-

Table 8
Farms in the Shelswell Group 1852-1939 per trade directories

Village	1852	1876	1911	1924	150 + acres	1939	150 + acres
Cottisford	2	2	2	3		2	1
Finmere	7	7	7	7	5	5	3
Fringford	7	7	7	6	3	6	1
Godington	5	5	4	4		4	4
Hardwick (Note 1)	2	2	2	2	1	2	2
Hethe	3	3	6	5	1	5	1
Mixbury	5	5	5	7	6	6	6
Newton Purcell (Note 2)	4	5	5	4	4	4	4
Stoke Lyne	7	6	6	5	4	6	6
Stratton Audley	9	8	6	6	6	7	5
Total	51	50	50	49	30	47	33

<u>Farm Names</u>

Cottisford	Cottisford, Heath, Manor.
Finmere	Bacon's House, Finmere Grounds, Glebe, Gravel, Hill Leys, Tile House, Town, Warren, Widmore.
Fringford	Eton College (later Church Farm), Fringford House, Fringford Mill, Glebe, Hall, Laurels, Manor, Waterloo.
Godington	Glebe, Hall, Moat, Poodle, Tithe.
Hardwick	Manor, Pimlico.
Hethe	Glebe, Hethe Brede, Manor, Montague, The Green, Willaston.
Mixbury	Cold Harbour, Fulwell, Home, Lodge, Middle, Monks House.
Newton Purcell	Barleyfields, Elm, Home, Newton Grange, Newton Morrell.
Stoke Lyne	Bainton, Baynards Green, Church, Home, Lower, Kilby's Barn, Manor, Park, Round Hill.
Stratton Audley	Elm, Oldfields, Pool, Stratton Audley Hall, Stratton Audley Manor, Stratton Audley Park, Willows.

<u>Farm Acreage</u>

1851-61 The acreage of the Fringford farms varied from 50 to over 500 acres.

1871 The acreage on the Fringford farms varied from 50 to 275 acres.

1924-39 It was only in these years that the trade directories indicated which farms had over 150 acres. It is noticeable that Fringford and Hethe had fewer farms with over 150 acres.

2008 Fringford's only active farm has some 1800 acres.

Notes

1. Hardwick includes Tusmore.

2. Newton Purcell includes Shelswell.

ments were created at the time of enclosure in 1854, and these survive as do those in Hethe. However, the most significant contributor to the labourers' menu was the family pig, which 'was everybody's pride and everybody's business.' 'During its lifetime the pig was an important member of the family, and its health and condition were regularly reported in letters to children away from home, together with news of their brothers and sisters. Men callers on Sunday afternoons came, not to see the family, but the pig.' After the killing by the pig-sticker, 'It was a busy time, but a happy one, with the larder full and something over to give away, and all the pride and importance of owning such riches.'[6]

The first decade of the twentieth century was a good one for the farmers, with the first rise in men employed on the farms since the 1860s. However, wages did not rise as much as prices and labourers were not as well off as, for example, casual dockers. In 1914, a landmark agreement was achieved at Sandringham: 'The King's Pay and The King's Conditions', which included sixteen shillings per week, a Saturday half-holiday and six-month tenancies for cottages. This may not have come into place elsewhere immediately but it did set a benchmark. After the Great War, times were hard in the 1920s and 1930s and jobs were scarce, leaving wages very little changed.

Tradesmen

In the late nineteenth and early twentieth centuries, the principal tradesmen and craftsmen in the villages were blacksmiths, boot/shoe makers, carpenters, tailors and wheelwrights. As the number of horses on the land declined, blacksmiths turned their skills to repairing agricultural machinery and cars. Similarly, coachmen adapted to become chauffeurs and mechanics, and stables became garages. The Motor House at Tusmore, built in 1902, was one of the first. Boot/shoemakers suffered from the competition in Northampton and by the 1930s only Fringford and Hethe had one recorded in the trade directories. Other trades suffered similarly from the rise in mass-produced goods and declining local markets. In many respects, however, the Shelswell villages remained self-sufficient until well after the Second World War, as we shall see in discussing village shops and post offices.

Women's employment

'It was often the women who felt most keenly the attraction of a new life in the towns. As they started to go into towns for their shopping on a

Saturday so they became more aware of the different, more exciting existence that awaited them there.'[7] By the end of the nineteenth century, many of the old country occupations, which had once kept women busy and provided additional money, had gone or were in serious decline. The growth of mass-produced goods, like glove-making (Worcester), lace making (Nottingham), and stockings (Leicester), sounded the death-knell for these cottage industries.

In 1900, 35% of all women over 15 were in paid employment, but only 10% of married women. There were many new jobs for women but they were mainly middle-class; for example, typists, telephone operators, physicians, bookkeepers, civil servants, the post office or in the new ABC Refreshment Rooms. In the villages, the main jobs were still limited to domestic service, dressmaking and school teaching. However, this did not stop some women, like Miss Lane in Fringford or Ann Bennett in neighbouring Fritwell (see below), taking over a smithy, pub or carrier's business, or running the post office or a small shop. The major changes in women's employment only came well after the Second World War, with increasing numbers entering the professions and working in the City.

Village shops and post offices[8]

If we look back to the 1820s and 1830s, most villages in the country had a shop of some kind. By the 1850s, the village shop was likely to be trading as a grocer and general shopkeeper. In addition, there was often a variety of smaller shops, which might not appear in the trade directories or the census returns. In Lark Rise, the innkeeper ran a small shop at the back of his premises, and the children used to knock at the back door to buy candles or treacle or cheese.[9] Even in Flora's day, there was competition for these village shops from traders in the local towns and the problem of declining rural populations. We shall see below the importance of the local carrier as a shopping agent. We should also remember that there were all manner of deliveries made to the villages, initially by horse and cart, and later in vans.

Many of the small shops survived until well after the Second World War. In Fringford, for example, in the 1950s you could still buy sweets, tobacco and cigarettes from Lizzie Grantham or 'Granny Wright', and groceries from Mrs Omar, whose sister ran the pub in Hethe. The shop closed in the late 1970s. In Hethe, Joseph Morgan, who was the local tailor, opened the post office and shop in the 1880s and the Morgan family ran it until it closed in 1974. In 1936 Thomas Henry Allen opened a shop,

Above: Mrs Omar's shop on the left, with the Butchers Arms at the end, Fringford, 1950s. Note her Morris 8 and the sign for Eldorado ice cream. The shop closed in the late 1970s. (Sue Gahan)
Below:Hethe Post Office and Shop, which the Morgan family ran from the 1880s to 1974, postcard early 1960s. (Mary Morgan)

'T.H.Allen', on the Green in Hethe. After initially selling cycles, he developed a business in radio, and electrical and mechanical repairs. The shop closed in the late 1980s.

From the 1850s, the new post offices were often an important addition to a village shop's business, although the handling of the Royal Mail was not always entrusted to the village shop. As we have seen, Miss Lane, the

T.H. Allen cycle, radio and repair shop (note the Shell petrol pump), and the off-licence (Morrells Oxford Ales), The Green, Hethe. The shop was open from 1936 to the late 1980s, postcard early 1960s. (Mary Morgan)

postmistress at Candleford Green, had a blacksmith's and wheelwright's business. In the late nineteenth century, more of the post office contracts were awarded to shopkeepers, and more blacksmiths and others took up retailing alongside the post office business. Most of the Shelswell villages had their own post office-cum-village shop. In the 1920s, local telephone exchanges were opened in the post offices and run on a manual basis by the postmistress. This gave her great scope to listen in to all the calls, so you had to watch what you said! Automatic exchanges replaced the manual ones about 1960. There were very few telephones until after the Second World War, most of them for the gentry and a few for local tradesmen.

The amount of official business, including the payment of old age pensions, given to these village shops with post offices, ensured that they remained profitable. By the 1980s, however, most of the shops/post offices in the Shelswell villages, together with the bakers, butchers and grocers, had closed, unable to resist the competition from Tesco and the other supermarkets. Even the enormous Dews' Store in neighbouring Fritwell, possibly the largest village shop in the country, had closed by 1980. Now there is just one shop in the ten villages, the recently opened Roots of Hardwick, a fine farm shop, which, unlike the supermarkets, offers everything fresh and without packaging. Long may it flourish! Another blow to many communities all over the country has been the closure of their pub, always a centre of village life. Five of the Shelswell villages are fortunate to still have a pub, a focal point now that so many village schools and shops have disappeared.

Country carriers

In the nineteenth century, or even earlier in some villages, if the local shops did not satisfy your needs, you could get a ride to one of the local towns with the country carrier. Every market day, he would set off from the village in the early morning and drive his horse and cart into town, setting off again in the mid-afternoon to be back home in the early evening. From the 1870s, for example, Jimmy Grantham of Fringford would call at Cottisford, Juniper Hill, Hethe and Stratton Audley on his weekly runs to market days at Banbury, Bicester, Brackley and Buckingham. Flora herself went to Banbury several times in his cart and makes reference to eating Banbury cakes. I have written elsewhere about carriers in the villages of Banburyshire.[10] The extent of Banbury's hinterland, linked by these carriers, was exceptional. In 1843, it was well defined by the editor of the *Banbury Guardian*: 'To the 140 places within a circuit of ten miles it may be said to be a metropolis'. Banbury's influence extended well beyond this ten-mile circuit and there were many, like Jimmy Grantham, travelling some 15-20 miles for the Thursday Market Day.

Jimmy, who was listed as a baker and coal dealer in 1876, was succeeded by his son, William, who was still operating in the 1920s. By the 1930s, Bert Bourton and then Albert Taylor, who operated from Stoke Lyne, were only running services to Bicester. By then, motor omnibuses had arrived on the scene and were operating daily services to Bicester, Buckingham and Oxford, and weekly ones to Banbury on Thursday market day. The other Shelswell villages either had their own carrier or one who passed their way. Finmere and Mixbury, for example, were served by Wilkinson, the Brackley to Buckingham carrier.

It was quite common for a carrier's business, like the Granthams', to be handed on from father to son. It was also common for a carrier to have another occupation like Jimmy Grantham, who was a baker and coal merchant. In neighbouring Fritwell, John Bennett, who kept the Bear Inn, was the carrier from 1864. By 1876, his widow, Ann, was the carrier, while a William Bennett ran the Bear. By 1911, John Bennett, presumably Ann's son, was the carrier and Ann was running the Bear. John was still the carrier in 1924. Similarly, in King's Sutton, William Barber was the carrier from about 1864 to 1906. He was succeeded by his son, William Edward, who continued until 1939. This continuity prevailed in other occupations, like blacksmiths (Plumbs of Fringford), and shop/post office (Morgans of Hethe and Stevens of Stratton Audley). There are also numerous examples of farms being handed on from father to son and then to grandson or granddaughter, like the Taylors of Waterloo Farm, Fringford, the Mansfields of Hethe Brede, and the Adams of Lower Farm, Stoke Lyne.

A ride with the carrier was cheap at a penny or two (only family members travelled free) but it was also slow and rather uncomfortable. However, the carrier also acted as a shopping agent, so that you could give him your list and he would bring the items back to you on his return. Many considered this well worthwhile in view of the wider range of goods available in the towns. Some carriers would even bring goods, like shoes, on approval. In many cases, payment was on tick and you paid the carrier what you could afford. It seems that carriers and shopkeepers tended to be generous to the poorer families and local pressures were such that there were few bad debts.

Travel

Railways

By the 1850s, Thomas Cook was taking serious tourists in large groups to France. However, it was not until the 1870s and the Bank Holiday Act of 1871, followed by the Cheap Trains Act of 1883, that significant numbers began to travel by train. Day trips to the seaside became a big annual event, particularly, for example, when the factories in Birmingham closed in August. There are local memories of some twenty trains coming then through Aynho on their way to Southsea or Weymouth on the south coast. Nellie Stockford of Lower Heyford, who died recently aged 106, remembered catching the 4am train from the station there to Weymouth every summer and returning late in the evening. There were regular advertisements for excursions in the *Bicester Advertiser*. In 1888, for example, there was an Intended Excursion from Bicester and neighbourhood on Monday 14 July 'to give 10 hours at Rhyl or Llandudno for 6s and a 3 day stay for 8s; 6 days 9s 6d. Train will probably start from Oxford, Bicester etc about 4am.'!

The only station in the Shelswell area was Finmere on the Great Central Railway (GCR), the last main line to be built and the first to be closed. The line opened on 15 March 1899 and closed on 3 September

Reuben Judd and his sons in Newton Purcell, possibly on their way from Fringford to collect coal from Finmere Station, early 1900s. (David Judd)

1966, following the proposals of Dr Beeching in 1962. Soon after the opening, Paxton & Holiday developed a live stock market on land adjacent to the station and work on the Shelswell Inn began in May 1900. The GCR was absorbed by the London & North Eastern Railway in 1923, and, on nationalisation in 1948, the line became part of the London Midland Region. Local coal merchants, like Reuben Judd and his sons of Fringford, used to collect their coal from the station. During the Second World War, Finmere saw frequent rail movements due to its close proximity to the airfields and military camps. Prisoners of War were marched from the station to the camp at the crossroads between Water Stratford and Stowe. As we have seen above, the station was also important for the Bicester Hunt.

Penny-Farthings to Porsches

Flora noted another major development in transport 'when the new low safety bicycle superseded the old penny-farthing type'.[11] The new Raleigh bicycle revolutionised cycling in the 1880s and 1890s, particularly for women. Cycling had been looked upon as a passing craze but in a few years 'there would be at least one bicycle in every one of their houses.'[12] Women's dress was also revolutionised and even if the village women did not wear Amelia Bloomer's new design of women's trousers, they were able to leave most of their petticoats behind in the bedroom.[13] The peak of the craze for cycling came in 1895-7, with 750,000 cycles produced annually. Photographs of women in the early 1900s quite often show them with their new prized bicycle. This allowed them to 'lightly mount 'the old bike' and pedal away to the market town to see the shops.'[14] The new bicycles also opened up opportunities for men to travel further for work. In the 1920s, some men locally used to cycle to London for work on a Monday and cycle back on a Friday, while others cycled at least as far as Coventry looking for work.

The next development was the motorcycle, which opened up further possibilities for both men and women from the 1920s. There are many photographs of them with their proud owners in the 1920s and 1930s, often with sidecars. These were ideal for girlfriends or members of the family or to carry your tools for work. I have even seen a photograph of a mobile smithy attached to a sidecar. Although cars had been around since the 1890s, only a few could afford them in this period. In Fringford, for example, there were only three cars in the 1930s. Now you can see one, two or more cars outside every house in the villages. The cyclists and 'bikers' of the 1920s, to say nothing of Flora, would be amazed to see the occasional gleaming Porsche or Bentley parked in their villages. Apart from all the parked cars, this dependence on the car means that demand for public transport is much reduced and, consequently, there are very limited rural bus services — a real problem for villagers who do not own a car.

The friendly societies

The friendly societies were formed to provide some insurance against accident, illness and death for the working classes, before the introduction of National Insurance in 1911. Between 1850 and 1875 there was a spectacular increase in the number of these societies, together with that of allied institutions like savings banks. By the end of the nineteenth century, there were some 27,000 registered friendly societies and thousands more that were not registered. In the first half of the nineteenth century, the authorities had been suspicious of such societies, because of their secret passwords and ceremonies. By the 1870s, however, self-help had become an approved form of social progress, and the government had acknowledged the role of the friendly societies and was encouraging membership. This membership came largely from the lower middle down into the lower classes.[15]

Locally, these societies have suddenly become of great interest, with the rediscovery in Fringford village hall of a beautiful silk Oddfellows' banner. At the same time, a certificate came to light, hanging unnoticed on a passage wall. This was issued on the formation of the Mansfield Lodge of the Independent Order of the Oddfellows (Manchester Unity) on 25th January, 1875. This has led to some enthusiastic research into the Oddfellows and other friendly societies and their banners, including contacts with the National Museum of Labour in Manchester and various other local Oddfellows' societies. The Mansfield connection was almost certainly with the family who were farming at Hall Farm in Fringford from the 1850s until the late 1930s.

The Oddfellows Friendly Society has a lengthy history, possibly dating back to 1452. However, in modern times, the key date was the formation of the Manchester Unity Order of Odd Fellows in 1813. By 1850, this Order had become the largest and richest friendly society in Britain. By 1911, when Asquith's Liberal Government passed the National Insurance Act, the Oddfellows protected so many people that the government used their actuarial tables to work out the level of contribution and payment required. At this time the Oddfellows was the largest friendly society in the world.

The Fringford banner is of particular interest, as it was made by George Tutill (1817-87) from Howden in the East Riding of Yorkshire. He set up business there in 1837 but by 1857 he had established himself in East London, where there was a large colony of silk-weavers. Over the years, his business was to manufacture more trade union banners than any other in the world, but it was not confined to trade unions. He also made banners and regalia for the Comical Fellows, Free Gardeners, Masons, Bands of Hope, Rechabites, Orange lodges and every kind of friendly society, including the Oddfellows. The regalia included sashes, emblems, aprons, collars and even robes and false beards for the United Ancient Order of Druids![16]

A special feature of his work was to have a different painting and inscription on the flip side of the banner, as we found on our banner, with 'All Men Are Brethren' inscribed on one side and 'United We Stand Divided We Fall' on the other. The colours of the banner are still sparkling, as it is has been kept in the original Tutill box. We were also fortunate to have an old photograph from about 1900-10, showing the banner in procession outside Fringford church. Most banners were put away after the defeat of Labour in the Great Strike of 1926, and discussion with some of the older residents seems to indicate that this banner was not carried in procession much after 1920.[17]

The Oddfellows' procession leaving Fringford church on feast day, on its way to enjoy the entertainment on the Green c.1900-10. (Bill Plumb)

It is impossible to know exactly when the Mansfield Lodge purchased the Tutill banner. For a small branch it would have been a major commitment and a major aspiration, costing about £55 in 1890. In the late 1880s, there was 'an orgy of banner-making', reaching a climax in 1889 with the great dockers' strike. Tutills were besieged, for with a Tutill banner, 'a branch *arrived*.'[18] So it is likely that the Mansfield Lodge made the commitment about this time. It was then too that Flora's father, Albert Timms, was a member of the Brackley Rock of Hope Branch of the Oddfellows, which had a monthly club night where he found the talk stimulating.[19] He paid 2s 6d per month and claimed sick pay on a number of occasions.

Flora commented that 'other, more conventional fraternities used at that time to say that the Oddfellows were no better than a lot of old freemasons and this idea was not discouraged by the Oddfellows themselves.' They liked to think of themselves as a secret society and most of the brethren were Liberals with a Radical tinge; 'altogether the Oddfellows were regarded as a daring lot; though, strange as it may appear to some people, their lives were generally exemplary.'[20] Although Fringford was a very conservative and controlled village, I doubt whether the squire or the rector were too troubled by the formation of an Oddfellows lodge. By the 1870s the Oddfellows and other friendly societies would have seemed quite respectable, and even been encouraged.

The minutes of the Mansfield Lodge from 1933 to 1966 have also come to light in the Oxfordshire Record Office. They show that members of the committee regularly attended the District AGM in Banbury or Buckingham. Sadly, they do not give any indication of the number of members, although a decrease in membership is noted as early as 1935. Neighbouring Tingewick had some 300 members and the Mansfield Lodge may well have had a similar number. There is evidence that membership was not confined to Fringford. Hardwick, Hethe, Juniper Hill and Stratton Audley all seem to have been involved, while Stoke Lyne had their own friendly society by the early 1900s. In 1949, the Mansfield Lodge moved its headquarters from Fringford (probably in the Old Rectory barn) to the old Hethe village hall, opposite the church. There are no minutes from 31 October 1956 to 21 April 1964, when the committee finally agreed to amalgamate with the Loyal Cherwell Valley Lodge, based in Deddington. On 5 April 1966, the Lodge closed, with 'the finances in very good position.' The Cherwell Valley Lodge later merged with a Banbury lodge.

The surviving minutes of the Lodge do not provide any details of the membership or their contributions and benefits. However, the neighbouring Grenville Lodge of the Oddfellows in Buckingham, which was formed in 1842, has records going back to 1857. These records provide details of contributions and benefits and the occupations of the members. Although the Grenville Lodge was much larger, it was also a member of the Banbury District, and its records are therefore an invaluable guide to the operations of the Mansfield Lodge. In 1880 the Lodge had some 80 members but by 1911 this had increased to about 800. In these early years, sickness benefit for the first 52 weeks was 12s and 6s thereafter, and funeral benefit £20. After the National Insurance Act of 1911, a new scale of contributions and benefits was set. In 1919 further new tables were introduced, which included an annuity after the age of 70. By 1940 there is evidence that most new members were joining from a Juvenile Lodge, aged 16, no doubt many of them the sons of members. The last member, number 1469, was admitted on 5 December 1974.

The listings of the male occupations serve to prove the earlier statement that membership of the friendly societies came largely from the lower middle down into the lower classes. Shoemaker, baker, coalman, painter, groom, carpenter, tailor, blacksmith and hurdle maker are just a few of the occupations listed. It is interesting to observe that, at least up to 1914, changes in individual occupations are noted. For example, tailor to collector of taxes, baker to farmer, servant to poultry farmer, shop assistant to cycle agent, labourers to police constable and electrician, and many to jobs on the railway. These reflect men moving with the times and seeking to improve their prospects.

Buckingham also catered for female members of the Oddfellows. The surviving records of the Florence Nightingale Lodge of the Oddfellows (Manchester Unity) show that they admitted their first member on 6 June 1898. By 1919 there were 49 members listed. Most of the members were listed as housewife, with a few as domestic, cook, cashier, shop assistant, laundress or hairdresser. By 1947 there were 47 surviving members, by 1968 there were only seven, and now there is only one, who joined at birth. There was a natural decline in membership of all the friendly societies after the introduction of the National Health Service in 1948. However, there are still some 350 members in the Bedfordshire and Buckinghamshire lodges. The three remaining lodges in Banbury have merged with the Heart of England Lodge in Leamington, and the Chipping Norton branch has merged with North Gloucestershire. In the current climate of 'credit-crunch', we might wish to see the return of more self-help and the support which the Oddfellows and other friendly societies have provided for so many men and women.[21]

By a strange coincidence, Albert Timms' membership of the Oddfellows has not been the only link between them and Lark Rise. On 12 July 1937, at an auction in the Town Hall, Brackley, the Grenville Lodge bought the allotments in Juniper Hill and still own them today. The eight acres of allotments, with a rental charge of £3.4s.0d., had been created on 7 November 1854 at the time of enclosure. The rental charge has since been commuted for a lump sum. Allotments were seen as a good investment by the Oddfellows, as a means of helping the poor.

I hope that this chapter has given a flavour of some of the major changes in village life since Flora's childhood. It only remains to give some coverage to the two most dramatic events of the last century and consider their impact on the local communities.

Notes

1   Flora Thompson, *Lark Rise to Candleford*, 417.
2   Thompson, *Lark Rise,* 246.
3   Daily Telegraph Weekend, 27 December, 2008.
4   Thompson, *Lark Rise,* 246.

5   J. C. Blomfield, Deanery of Bicester, *Fringford*, 38.

6   Thompson, *Lark Rise*, 24-27.

7   G.E. Mingay, *Rural Life in Victorian England*, 191.

8   Jonathan Brown & Sadie Ward, *The Village Shop.*

9   Thompson, *Lark Rise*, 65.

10   M.W. Greenwood, *Villages of Banburyshire*, 12-13.

11   Thompson, *Lark Rise*, 476.

12   Thompson, *Lark Rise*, 255.

13   Thompson, *Lark Rise*, 477.

14   Thompson, *Lark Rise*, 255.

15   Geoffrey Best, *Mid-Victorian Britain 1851-75*, 291.

16   John Gorman, *Banner Bright*, 52.

17   Gorman, *Banner Bright*, 6-19.

18   Gorman, *Banner Bright*, 7.

19   Christine Bloxham, *The World of Flora Thompson Revisited*, 134.

20   Flora Thompson, *Still Glides the Stream*, 159-60.

21   I am indebted to Jean Nicholls for access to the records of the Buckingham Oddfellows' Lodges.

Chapter 7

The War Dead

'When you go home today, tell them of us and say,
For your today, we gave our tomorrow.'

The names on the war memorials and graves in the Shelswell villages are a stark reminder of just how many local men 'gave their tomorrows' in the two World Wars. They show what a devastating effect these wars had on families and their local communities. As a crucial aspect of village life during the last century, it seemed important to me to examine the available records of all these war dead and try to bring some life to the names. In many cases, the families are still around and there are still memories of the dead. I hope that in some small way the personal records, which are detailed below, may help them and us, our children and future generations to understand how devastating these losses were.

In some villages, the names are recorded on a war memorial, in others in the church, either as a group or individually, or simply on a gravestone in the churchyard. Given this information, it has generally been possible to find further details from the website of the Commonwealth War Graves Commission. However, in spite of my efforts and local enquiries, I am afraid there are still some gaps. It was only in Mixbury and Newton Purcell that they also listed all those who went to fight. In Mixbury, the list covers the 'Great War 1914-19', while in Newton Purcell, the list includes all those who went to fight in both World Wars. I have not included all these names.

It is also of interest to see the variety of places in which the two wars were fought, and the number of places where the dead are buried. These lists also show how shattering it must have been for families who lost more than one relative, like the Blaby, Cross and Peverell families of Cottisford and Juniper Hill, the Symes-Thompsons of Finmere, the Cokers of Fringford, the French family of Hethe, the Horwoods of Newton Purcell, the Peytons and Mays of Stoke Lyne, and the Ayris family of Stratton Audley.

As one who has visited some of the Commission's cemeteries in France, I have to say what a moving and memorable experience it is to see the rows of beautifully kept graves. Although the smaller cemeteries are in some ways the most moving, it is the splendour of the memorials at Thiepval, Tyne Cot and Vimy Ridge that most people will probably remember. The Commission has done, and is doing, a wonderful job in providing such a fitting tribute to all those who sacrificed their lives.

The information below includes, where possible, the following details of each casualty: full name, parents and widow (if any), rank and service number, battalion and regiment, date of death and age, and name of the cemetery or memorial where he is buried or commemorated, together with the Commission's reference number for the grave.

Cottisford and Juniper Hill

1914-18

John Blaby, son of Joseph and Alice Blaby, of Cottisford. Private 26607, 1st Battalion, Duke of Cornwall's Light Infantry, died 23 April 1917, age 27. La Chaudiere Military Cemetery, (north-east side of Vimy Ridge), Plot VI, Row D, Grave 10.

William Blaby, John's brother. Rifleman 40665, 1st Battalion, Royal Irish Rifles, died 1 April 1917, age 28. Fins New British Cemetery, Sorel-le-Grand (Somme), Plot VI, Row F, Grave 16.

Ernest Alfred Victor Blencowe, son of Harriet Blencowe (later Mrs Massey), of Juniper Hill. Private 143575, Machine Gun Corps (Infantry), died 15 April 1918, age 32. Le Grand Beaumart British Cemetery, Steenwerck (just west of Armentieres), Plot III, Row G, Grave 1.

Alfred Dennis Cross, son of John Thomas and Annie Elizabeth Cross, of Cottisford. Private G/23014, 10th Battalion, The Queen's (Royal West Surrey Regiment), died 20 September 1917, age 22. Tyne Cot Memorial (east of Ypres), Panel 15.

Leeman John Cross, Alfred's brother. Private 70751, Berkshire Yeomanry, died 27 November 1917, age 20. Jerusalem War Cemetery (3 miles north of the walled city), Panel 4.

Henry Patrick Farrer, of Cottisford, son of Luke and Julia Farrer, of Chelsea, and husband of Kate Elizabeth Pettit. Driver 61478, 94th Field Company, Royal Engineers, died 26 November 1918, age 41. St Sever Cemetery extension (south of Rouen), Block S, Plot III, Row B, Grave 2.

Sydney Gaskin, son of Joseph and Mary Lucy Gaskin, of Juniper Hill. L/Cpl 8468, 1st Battalion, Ox & Bucks Light Infantry, died at Adana, Southern Turkey on 27 September 1917. Baghdad (North Gate) War Cemetery, Plot XXI, Row W, Grave 28, Iraq.

Hubert Harris, son of Aloysius and Susannah Harris, of Juniper Hill. Sapper 34583,

26th Field Company, Royal Engineers, died 25 April 1916, age 23. St Patrick's Cemetery, Loos-en-Gohelle, Plot III, Row B, Grave 23.

Ernest Peverell, son of Ernest Thomas and Alice Peverell, of Kennel Cottages, Cottisford. Gunner 62381, Royal Field Artillery, 96th Battery, 19th Brigade, died 27 October 1918, age 22. Mikra British Cemetery, Kalamaria, Greece, Grave 682.

William Peverell, Ernest's brother. Private, Shropshire Light Infantry, died in Fringford in February 1919. Buried at Cottisford (stone cross in SW corner of the churchyard commemorates him and his brother).

Edwin Timms, son of Albert and Emma Timms, of Juniper Hill, and brother of Flora Thompson. Private 81889, 2nd Battalion, Canadian Infantry (Eastern Ontario Regiment), died 26 April 1916, age 36. Woods Cemetery, Zillebeke, (just south of Ypres), Plot II, Row F, Grave 3. An inscription at the foot of his headstone, chosen by his mother Emma, reads "Thy way not mine O Lord".

1939-45

Ronald John Watts, son of George and Ellen Watts, of Juniper Hill, and husband of Edna Watts, of Southwick, Wilts. Guardsman 2616522, 5th Battalion, Grenadier Guards, died February 1944, age 24. Cassino Memorial, Italy (just south of the Abbey on Monte Cassino), Panel 3.

Finmere

1914-18

Cholmeley Symes-Thompson, son of the late Dr Edmund and Elizabeth Symes-Thompson, and husband of Grace, of Kensington. Captain, 2nd Battalion, Grenadier Guards, died 17 November 1914, age 33. Zillebeke Churchyard (just south of Ypres), Row F, Grave 2.

Wilfred Paxton, L/Cpl 220081, Royal Berkshire Regiment, died 15 February 1918. Tyne Cot Memorial (Ypres), Panel 105 to 106 and 162.

Herbert Bignell, Private 8578, 2nd Battalion, Northamptonshire Regiment, died 14 March 1915. Le Touret Memorial, Pas de Calais, Panel 28 to 30.

Archibald Clifford, son of John and Ann Clifford, of Lower End, Finmere, and husband of Elizabeth Clifford, of Leeds. Private 5762, 2nd Battalion, Ox & Bucks Light Infantry, died 16 May 1915, age 34. Le Touret Memorial, Pas de Calais, Panel 26.

Frank Clifford, son of Harry and Elizabeth Clifford, of Finmere. Private 19638, 2nd Battalion, Wiltshire Regiment, died 1 July 1916, age 21. Thiepval Memorial (Somme), Panel (Pier and Face) 13A.

William Clifford, son of Thomas 'Tommy-Dodd' and Margaret Clifford, of Finmere. Private SD/659, 11th Battalion, Royal Sussex Regiment, died 3 September 1916, age 26. Thiepval Memorial (Somme), Panel (Pier and Face) 7C.

George Frederick Davis, son of Thomas and Louisa Davis of Shoreditch, London.

Private 5769, 1st/4th Battalion, Royal Fusiliers, died 12 October 1916, age 36. St Sever Cemetery (south of Rouen), Block B, Row 14, Grave 33.

1939-45

Benjamin Robert Buck, son of Albert and Hannah Buck, and husband of Olive Alice Buck, of Finmere. Gunner 1427327, Royal Artillery (HQ.6 H.A.A. Regiment), died 29 November 1942, age 27, a POW at Fukuoka, Japan. Yokohama Cremation Memorial, Panel 2.

Douglas John Bull, son of Frank and Sophia Bull, of Finmere. Private 5961893, 2nd Battalion, Beds & Herts Regiment, died 6 May 1943, age 20. Medjez-el-Bab Cemetery, Tunisia, Plot 2, Row G, Grave 9.

George Horwood, son of John and Alice Horwood of Little Tingewick. Gunner 1712406, 80th Field Regiment, Royal Artillery, died 25 April 1945, age 35, just seven days before the cessation of fighting on 2 May. Becklingen War Cemetery, Germany, Plot 4, Row L, Grave 4. This cemetery overlooks Luneburg Heath, where Field Marshall Montgomery accepted the German surrender on 4 May 1945.

Dr Richard Edmund Symes-Thompson, son of Dr and Mrs H.E.Symes-Thompson of Finmere House. Wounded in an air raid and died at St Luke's Hospital in Chelsea on 11 May 1941. Buried at Finmere.

Fringford

1914-18

Frederick James Batchelor, son of Robert and Anne Batchelor of Green Farm, Fringford. Private 306529, 1st/8th Battalion, Royal Warks Regiment, died 27 August 1917, age 23. Tyne Cot Memorial (Ypres), Panel 23 to 28 and 163A.

John William Gerring, son of James (Jimmy) and Jane Gerring, of Main Street, Fringford. Private 84598, 11th Company, Machine Gun Corps (Infantry), died 22 December 1917, age 23. Windmill British Cemetery, Monchy-le-Preux, Pas de Calais, Plot 1, Row H, Grave 8. Jimmy Gerring was the church sexton for many years.

Charles Thomas Marriott, Private 201893, 2nd/4th Battalion, Ox & Bucks Light Infantry, died 21 March 1918, age 21. Pozieres Memorial, nr. Albert, Panel 50 and 51. A Mrs Marriott was a sister of Jimmy Gerring, so Charles Marriott and John Gerring were probably cousins.

Charles Ernest Richardson, son of Charles and Mary Richardson, of Fringford. Private 4509, Royal Warks Regiment, died 9 October 1917, age 21. Tyne Cot Memorial (Ypres), Panel 23 to 28 and 163A.

Alfred Waring, son of Henry and Jemima Waring, of Fringford, and husband of Mrs A.Waring of Rectory Cottage, Tingewick, Bucks. Private 968, Royal Bucks Hussars, died 21 August 1915, age 38. Helles Memorial, Gallipoli Peninsula, Turkey, Panel 16 and 17.

Four other men who died in the Great War or the Boer War are commemorated in the church. Two of them were members of the Revd Coker's family. Their names are recorded on the plaques below the second window in the north aisle, which was dedicated to the Cokers in 1898:

Cadwallader John Coker, younger son of James Gould and Florence Emily Coker, of Mayfield, Sussex. Lt, Welsh Regiment, killed in action at St Eloi, 22 June 1915, age 23. Ridge Wood Military Cemetery, Dickebusch, Flanders, Plot 1, Row E, Grave 1.

Alexander Y. Crawshay Mainwaring Spearman, husband of Jessie Aubrey Loch (formerly Spearman), of Crediton, Devon, daughter of the Revd Cadwallader Coker. Commander, Collingwood Battalion, R.N.D. Killed in action in the Dardanelles, 4 June 1915, age 52. Helles Memorial, Gallipoli Peninsula, Turkey, Panel 1 and 2.

The third man is commemorated in the first window in the north aisle. He was a member of the squire's family and died during the Boer War:

Edward John Dewar, Captain 60th Rifles, died 20 February 1900 of wounds received in action at Paardeburg, South Africa, while serving with the Mounted Infantry, age 36.

The fourth man is commemorated on a plaque by the south door. He was the brother of Mrs Ellis Chinnery:

James Dixon, son of Mr J. Dixon, of Kensington. Captain (Adjutant), 2nd Battalion, Middlesex Regiment, fell in action at Neuve Chapelle, 10 March 1915, age 30. Royal Irish Rifles Graveyard, Laventie, Pas de Calais, Plot III, Row K, Grave 4.

1939-45

John Edward Blake (always known as Jack), son of Walter and Anne Blake and husband of Elsie Nellie Blake, of Twyford, Bucks. Private 105892529, R.O.A.C., died 15 March 1945, age 37. Buried at Schoonselhof Cemetery, Antwerp, Plot IV, Row B, Grave 1.

Gordon John Hancock, son of Hubert Gerald and Constance Annie Hancock of Eaton Socon, Bucks. Driver T/5383004, 18 Supply Group, R.A.S.C., died 25 July 1943, a POW, age 23. Kanchanaburi War Cemetery, Thailand (129 km NW of Bangkok), Plot 4, Row A, Grave 50.

Godington

1914-18

W.A.G. Webb, Private 16346, 8th Battalion, Ox & Bucks Light Infantry, died 17 July 1915. Buried at Godington.

Hardwick

1939-45

Ronald William Wyatt, son of Cyril and Annie Wyatt, husband of Lucy Annie Wyatt. Private 5956759, 9th Battalion, Beds & Herts Regiment, died 3 January 1946, age 31. Buried at Hardwick.

Hethe

1914-18

Fell in Action

H.G.Watkin, son of Col.H.Watkin CB. Major, 4th (Queen's Own) Hussars; Brigade Major, 2nd Midland Mounted Brigade, died 21 August 1915, age 41. Helles Memorial Cemetery, Gallipoli Peninsula, Turkey, Addenda Panel 204.

C. Adams, L/Cpl 10295, 5th Battalion, Ox & Bucks Light Infantry, died 25 September 1915, age 17. Harlebeke New British Cemetery, Belgium, Plot XII, Row A, Grave 16.

Edwin Francis Lane, son of James and Agnes Lane, of Hethe. Private 19642, 1st Battalion, Wiltshire Regiment, died 6 June 1915, age 17. Ypres Memorial (Menin Gate), Panel 53.

J.W. Fathers, Private 48601, 5th Battalion, Royal Berks Regiment, died 26 August 1916. Peronne Road Cemetery, Maricourt (Somme), Plot III, Row C, Grave 33.

Harold Alfred French, son of James and Ellen French, of Hethe, Trooper 285306, Queen's Own Oxfordshire Hussars, died 1 April 1918, age 22. Moreuil Communal Cemetery Allied Extension (Somme), Row C, Grave 7.

P. French, Harold's brother. ?RMLI.

F. Smith, Private 8877, 2nd Battalion, Dorsetshire Regiment, died 29 August 1916, age 23. Baghdad (North Gate) War Cemetery, Iraq, Plot XXI, Row T, Grave 29.

William Arthur Trafford, son of Willoughby Trafford of Coneygre Farm, Hethe. Private 12533, 5th Battalion, Ox & Bucks Light Infantry, died 25 September 1915. Ypres Memorial (Menin Gate), Panel 37 and 39.

Died

A. Langford, Private, Worcs Regiment.

G. Meads, Private, Canadian Regiment ?

W. Stevens, Private 6163, 1st Battalion, Royal Warks Regiment, died 19 December 1917. Brookwood Military Cemetery, Plot XIII, Row E, Grave 5B.

1939-45

Henry Pyers Ronald Lloyd-Mostyn, son of Col. M.L. & Mrs Margaret Eleanor Lloyd-Mostyn, of The Old Vicarage, Hethe. 2/Lt 85587, Royal Armoured Corps, 15/19th Hussars, died 27 May 1940. Dunkirk Memorial, Column 4.

Oliver George Wakefield, Private 14558952, 1st Wiltshire Regiment, died 11 August 1945, age 21. Karachi War Cemetery, Plot 12, Row A, Grave 16.

Mixbury

1914-18 (29 listed as going to fight)

E.H. Blencowe, son of Thomas and Hannah Blencowe, of Mixbury. Private 10695, 5th Battalion, Ox & Bucks Light Infantry, died 24 June 1915, age 21. Bailleul Communal Cemetery Extension (Nord), France, Plot I, Row D, Grave 12.

Leslie H. Paxton, Sgt 10674, 5th Battalion, OBLI, died 12 July 1915. Poelcapelle British Cemetery, Belgium, Plot LVII, Row D, Grave 12.

Reginald Strickland, son of Elizabeth and the late William Strickland, of Mixbury. 2/Lt, 3rd Battalion, Ox & Bucks Light Infantry, died 25 December 1915, age 23. Bethune Town Cemetery (north of Arras), Plot II, Row L, Grave 5.

1939-45

John Richard St Leger Aldworth, son of Major J.C.O. and Mrs L.S.C.Aldworth, of Mixbury Hall and County Cork, and husband of Margaret Jean Aldworth. Major 117163, 2nd Battalion, Royal Ulster Rifles, died 10 June 1944, age 29. La Delivrande War Cemetery, Douvres (north of Caen), Plot IX, Row D, Grave 2.

This cemetery was opened after the Normandy landings on 6 June 1944.

Robert Henry Dunkley, son of John Geoffrey and Alice Mary Dunkley of Northampton, Sergeant (Air Gunner) 1608128, 17 September 1944, age 20. Buried at Mixbury.

Newton Purcell

1914-18 (25 listed as going to fight)

Leonard Holton, Private 14598, 18th (Queen's Mary's Own) Hussars, died 20 November 1917, age 30. Cambrai Memorial, Louverval, Panel 1.

John Horwood DCM, probably Oliver's brother. L/Cpl 9037, Ox & Bucks Light Infantry, died 3 September 1916. Baghdad (North Gate) War Cemetery, Iraq, Plot XXI, Row D, Grave 23.

Oliver Horwood, son of Edward and Harriet Horwood, of 21 Newton Purcell. Private 8592, 1st Battalion, Scots Guards, died 29 October 1914. Ypres Memorial (Menin Gate), Panel 11.

1939-45 (12 listed as going to fight)

Harold Gough, of Warins Barn, Shelswell (uncle of Walter Gough). Gunner, Royal Artillery. Died as a POW in the Far East, probably on the Burma Road.

Stoke Lyne

1914-18

Henry S.C. Peyton, MC, son of Sir Algernon Peyton, 6th Bt. and Lady Peyton of Delaford Manor, Iver, Bucks. Lt/Col, Commanding 2nd Battalion, Rifle Brigade, died 24 March 1918, age 26. Fouquescourt British Cemetery (east of Amiens), Plot I, Row E, Grave 1.

William Clarence May, son of Thomas and Elizabeth Hannah May of Baynards Green. 2/Lt, 1st/5th Battalion, Northumberland Fusiliers, died 26 October 1917, age 25. Tyne Cot Memorial (Ypres), Panel 19 to 23 and 162.

Howard Stanley May, brother of William. Private 200931, 2nd/4th Ox & Bucks Light Infantry, died 22 August 1917, age 21. Tyne Cot Memorial (Ypres), Panel 96 to 98.

Charles W. Butler, son of Mrs R.Butler of Stoke Lyne. Private 17159, 2nd Hampshire Regiment, died 20 November 1915. Buried at Alexandria (Chatby) Military and War Memorial Cemetery, Row B, Grave 115.

Cecil Arthur Brandrick, son of Mr and Mrs J. Brandrick, and husband of Caroline Eleanor Usher Brandrick, of Stratford on Avon. Private 18495, 11th Royal Warks Regiment, died 28 August 1916, age 24. Wimereux Communal Cemetery, nr. Boulogne, Plot I, Row P, Grave 25A.

Gilbert Collins, son of Thomas and Eliza Collins, of Stoke Lyne. Private 17404, 5th Battalion, Ox & Bucks Light Infantry, died 22 August 1917, age 21. Tyne Cot Memorial (Ypres), Panel 96 to 98.

W. Curtis, Private, Bucks Yeomanry, drowned off Alexandria 30 December 1917.

P.A. Damant, DSM, MSM, son of Allan John and Mary Ann Damant of Woodbine Cottage, Stoke Lyne. Private 19157, 1st Kent Cyclists, 10th Battalion, Queen's Own (Royal West Kent Regiment), died 27 April 1918, age 30. Hagle Dump Cemetery, Belgium, Plot I, Row D, Grave 11.

William M. Golder, son of Mr and Mrs Alfred Golder, of Stoke Lyne Cottages, and husband of Clara N.Golder, of Charlbury. Native of Stoke Lyne. Private 24231, 2nd Royal Warks Regiment, died 20 October 1917, age 30. Etaples Military Cemetery, Pas de Calais, Plot XXX, Row E, Grave 17. This was the largest Commission cemetery in France, designed by Sir Edwin Lutyens.

H.G. Hinton, son of Mrs Mary Hinton, of Stoke Lyne. Private 14411, 7th Wiltshire Regiment, died 20 October 1916, age 24. Pieta Military Cemetery, nr. Valletta, Malta, Plot D, Row XIII, Grave 6.

1939-45

John Henry Peyton, son of Sir Algernon Peyton, 7th Bt and Lady Peyton, of Bicester. Lt 256086, 12th (2nd Battalion, The Queen's Westminsters) Battalion, King's Royal Rifle Corps, died 13 April 1945, age 21. Becklingen War Cemetery, Germany, Plot 4, Row K, Grave 3. This cemetery overlooks Luneburg Heath, where Field-Marshal Montgomery accepted the German surrender on 4 May 1945.

Stratton Audley

1914-19

Albert Ayris, son of Robert and Hannah Ayris, of Stratton Audley. Private S/10228, 1st Battalion, Seaforth Highlanders, died 7 January 1916, age 31. Basra Memorial, Iraq, Panel 37 and 64.

Thomas Henry Ayris, Albert's brother. Private 288883, Queen's Own Oxfordshire Hussars, died 21 June 1917. Templeux-le-Guerard British Cemetery, Plot II, Row E, Grave 46.

John Henry Cox, Private 39944, 10th Battalion, Worcs Regiment, died 18 November 1916. Thiepval Memorial (Somme), Panel (Pier and Face) 11C.

William John Dagley.

James Henry Eyles, son of James and Eliza Herring, of Stratton Audley. Private 24191, 14th Battalion, Glos Regiment, died 10 June 1916, age 19. Merville Communal Cemetery, nr. Bethune, Plot VI, Row P, Grave 63.

Richard James House, son of George and Mary House, of Stratton Audley. Private 12722, 7th Battalion, Norfolk Regiment, died 8 August 1918, age 28. Morlancourt British Cemetery No.2, nr. Albert, Row A, Grave 20.

Ernest Arthur Norton, son of William and Emma Norton, of Stratton Audley. Rifleman A/445, 8th Battalion, King's Royal Rifle Corps, died 3 August 1915, age 25. Ypres Memorial (Menin Gate), Panel 51 and 53.

John Edward Stevens, son of Edward and Mary Laura Stevens, of Stratton Audley. Private 201635, 2nd/4th Battalion, Ox & Bucks Light Infantry, died 21 March 1918, age 22. Bellicourt British Cemetery, nr. St Quentin, Special Memorial, Row A, Grave 7.

Richard Thorpe, Private 17378, 11th Battalion, Royal Warks Regiment, died 13 August 1916. Thiepval Memorial (Somme), Panel (Pier and Face) 9A, 9B and 10B.

1939-45

Merton Beckwith-Smith, DSO, MC, of Aberader, son of Beckwith and Georgina, and husband of Honor, of Sulhamstead, Berks. Major General, Welsh Guards, Comd 1st Guards Brigade 1939-40; G.O.C.18th Infantry Div. 1940. Died 11 November 1942, a POW in the Far East, age 52. Sai Wan War Cemetery, Hong Kong, Plot V, Row H, Grave 1.

Norman Joseph Goss, son of Edward Arthur and Lizzie Goss, of Stratton Audley. Sgt (Air Bomber) 1318695, 106 Squadron, Bomber Command, RAF Voluntary Reserve, died 23 March 1944, age 22. Durnbach War Cemetery, Bad Tolz, Bavaria, Plot 8, Row F, Grave 15.

* * *

The total dead in the ten parishes was 60 in the Great War and 16 in the Second World War. However, fate dealt more cruelly with some parishes than others, particularly in the Great War. If you compare the list with the 1911 Census figures, Cottisford lost 11/150 or 1/14 and Hethe lost 11/296 or 1/26. Overall the Shelswell average was 1/45, compared to a national average of around 1/55. This does not of course take into account others who may have been seriously wounded or scarred in other ways. There were so many others who did not survive to lead happy and healthy lives.[1]

Perhaps the last moving words should come from Flora, as she stood in Cottisford church and remembered the deaths of her brother, Edwin (Edmund) and other local boys:

> 'And all the time boys were being born or growing up in the parish, expecting to follow the plough all their lives, or, at most, to do a little mild soldiering or go to work in a town. Gallipoli? Kut? Vimy Ridge? Ypres? What did they know of such places? But they were to know them, and when the time came they did not flinch. Eleven out of that tiny community never came back. A brass plate on the wall of the church, immediately over the old end house seat is engraved with their names. A double column, five names long, then, last and alone, the name of Edmund.'[2]

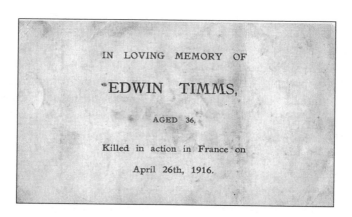

IN LOVING MEMORY OF

"EDWIN TIMMS,

AGED 36,

Killed in action in France on
April 26th, 1916.

Notes

1 I am indebted to Ted Flaxman for the figures in this paragraph.
2 Flora Thompson, *Lark Rise to Candleford*, 247.

Chapter 8

Conclusion

'You are goin' to be loved' she said, 'loved by a lot o' folks – strangers shall become friends – people all over –' and she waved her bundle of wood-sage to include the entire horizon.[1]

This was the gipsy woman's prophecy after the young Flora had helped her find medicinal wood-sage in the woods. If ever a prophecy could be said to have come true, this must be it, particularly with the advent of the BBC television series. I hope that what I have written may help in some small way to put the series into perspective and shed some light on daily life in Lark Rise country during and after Flora's Victorian childhood. I hope too that the series will encourage many viewers to go back to Flora's books or to read them for the first time. I am enormously grateful that it has been my good fortune to live in Candleford Green and come under the spell of Flora. As 'a child of poverty', she had a unique gift in being able to put her life and the lives of her villages into perspective. She was also able, as one of the past rectors wrote, 'to describe the hypocrisy of the clergy and the arrogance of the gentry with a benign and gentle irony'.[2] She sheds light on so many aspects of rural life and she has certainly been the inspiration for me to look at some of the major changes in village life since her Victorian childhood.

It is a simple matter to reach this conclusion about the quality and relevance of Flora's work, which has provided a thread through all the previous chapters. For the rest, I suppose that there is no real conclusion to what I have written. The story of these villages is 'like an ever-flowing stream' in which we all swim for a brief while. As we have seen, much has changed but, as all local historians love to say, there is much evidence too of continuity. Church attendance may be at an all time low but the ten parishes still have their own churches. The Methodists may have disappeared from these villages but they can still be found in neighbouring

Fritwell, and the Roman Catholic chapel in Hethe still flourishes. Many of the village schools may have disappeared but most of the children still go to the two remaining primary schools. The 'great houses' may have changed hands and their estates may have diminished but their influence, though less, lives on. The number of farms has declined dramatically but the survivors have either adapted to change or explored other avenues. Last and by no means least, the Bicester and Warden Hunt continues strongly, in spite of the political pressures to ban hunting. Hunting has been part of our local heritage for centuries and it seems unlikely that any government intervention will put a stop to it.

Although the Shelswell Group still has ten churches open, their future must be uncertain. With declining church attendance and a shortage of clergy, it is becoming increasingly difficult for the Benefice to maintain and service ten churches and for all the parishes to pay their shares to the Diocese. As Trevor Beeson says, there is a vital need for a new strategy. He suggests that the parishes should be allowed to nominate their own priest to serve within a predominantly lay ministerial community. In addition there should be a diocesan ministerial team of full-time priests and lay specialists who, under the direction of the bishop, would be available to the parishes for tasks such as the ordering of worship, education, youth work and particular pastoral problems. Will the Church of England surprise us and make some much-needed decisions along these lines? Or will it be left to the unsung parish priests and lay helpers to muddle along as best they can? Also, in the face of Islam and growing secularism, will greater unity emerge within the Church of England and closer communion with the Nonconformists and Roman Catholics?

For the future, many of us in the Shelswell villages may wish, like the Hobbit, for 'more green and less noise' but that is impossible, with the population projected to reach some 77 million by 2050. We may be spared an eco-town at Weston-on-the-Green but the green spaces between Stratton Audley and Bicester are likely to be filled by the development of Caversfield airfield. Similarly, the green spaces between Fringford and Bicester are also likely to be filled, initially by the development of Dymocks Farm. Will the future see many more of us living in apartments, as many of the continentals do, and houses too expensive for all except the very rich? In these difficult and uncertain times, both socially and economically, perhaps we should be looking back to the people of Lark Rise with their 'Don't flinch' and self-help attitude, and their determination to avoid the workhouse and dependence on parish/ public relief i.e.

the benefit system. At the same time, perhaps we should look forward to the future with 'the audacity of hope', the great phrase adopted by the newly elected President of the United States, Barack Obama.

Notes

1   Flora Thompson, *The Peverel Papers* quoted in *A Country Calendar,* 131.
2   John M. Sergeant, *A History of Fringford and Newton Purcell-cum-Shelswell.*

Bibliography

For those who may wish to explore the history of these villages further, I attach a list of the main primary and published sources which I have consulted.

Primary Sources
Census returns 1801-1901.
Parish registers.
W.Potts, *List and Directory (formerly J.G.Rusher's)* 1897-1906.
J.G. Rusher, *Rusher's Banbury's Lists and Directories* (1796-1896).
Trade directories, including *Gardner's, Harrods, Kelly's,* and *Post Office.*

Published Sources
Pauline Ashridge, *Village Chapels* (2004).
Peter Barrington, *The Changing Faces of Bicester, Book One* (1998).
Peter Barrington and David Watts, *The Changing Faces of Bicester, Book Two* (1999).
Peter Bushell, *Swift's House, Stoke Lyne, A History* (undated and not published).
Trevor Beeson, *Round the Church in 50 Years* (2007).
J.C. Blomfield, *Deanery of Bicester,* Part III (1887), Part V (1890/91), and Part VIII (1894).
Christine Bloxham, *The World of Flora Thompson Revisited* (2007).
Jonathan Brown & Sadie Ward, *The Village Shop* (1990).
Victoria Solt Dennis, *Discovering Friendly and Fraternal Societies, Their Badges and Regalia* (Shire Book 2005).
Finmere and Little Tingewick Historical Society, *The Millennium History of Finmere* (2001).
Ted & Joan Flaxman, *Cottisford Revisited* (1999, revised 2008).
John Gorman, *Banner Bright, An illustrated history of the banners of the British trade union movement* (1973).
Joy Grant, *Hethe-with-Adderbury, The story of a Catholic parish in Oxfordshire* (2000).

Ralph Greaves, *A Short History of the Bicester & Warden Hill Hunt* (c.1965).

Ralph Greaves, *Foxhunting in Oxfordshire, Berkshire and Buckinghamshire* (1960s).

M.W. Greenwood, *Parishes, Parsons and Persuasions* (1997, not published).

M.W. Greenwood, *Fringford Through the Ages* (2000).

M.W. Greenwood, *Villages of Banburyshire, including Lark Rise to Candleford Green* (2006).

Pamela Horn, *The Rise and Fall of the Victorian Servant* (1975).

Gillian Lindsay, *Flora Thompson: The Story of the 'Lark Rise' Writer* (1990, revised 2008).

E.P. List, *Godington, The Story of an Oxfordshire village (2006).*

Albert Parker, *Four Shires,* April 2007 and January 2008.

Rev.C. Rayner-Smith, *Hardwick-cum-Tusmore* (1972).

The Rotary Club of Bicester, *The Bicester Story – Reflections of Town and Village* (1999).

John M. Sergeant, *A History of Fringford and Newton Purcell-cum-Shelswell* (1980s).

John M. Sergeant, *The Story of Hethe, Oxfordshire* (1980s).

Flora Thompson, *Lark Rise to Candleford* (Penguin 1973, reissued 2008).

Flora Thompson, *Still Glides the Stream* (1948).

Kate Tiller, *Church and Chapel in Oxfordshire* 1851: *The return of the census of religious worship,* Oxfordshire Record Society 55, 1987.

Victoria County History of Oxford, vi (Ploughley Hundred), 1959.

David Watts and Peter Barrington, *The Changing Faces of Bicester,* Books Three to Five (2000, 2001 and 2003).

Index

Adderbury, 35
Adelaide, Lady, see Slater-Harrison, Lady Cecilia
agriculture, 75-80, 106
Allan, Revd Donald, 25
Allen, Thomas Henry (T.H.), 83
allotments, 80-82
Annesley, Arthur, see Valentia, 11th Viscount
Arless, Caroline (Sue Braby), 15, 17

Bainton, 41, 51-52
Banbury, 49, 92, 93
Barber, family, carriers, 86-87
Barnett, Charles, 53
Barnett, family, 43
BBC television series, 13-22
Beckwith-Smith, Mrs, 60
Beeson, Trevor, 25, 29-31, 106
benefice, see Shelswell Benefice,
Bennett, family, carriers, 83, 86-87
Bicester, 14, 19, 49, 57, 60, 69, 106
Bicester Hall, 54
Bicester Hounds, 52, 61
Bicester Hunt, 49, 50-63, 88, 106
Bicester and Warden Hill Hunt, see Bicester Hunt
Bicester, 1st Lord, 45, 47, 62
Bicester, 2nd Lord, 47, 48
Blundell-Leigh, John, 59
Bourton, Bert, carrier, 86
Brabazon, John, 54, 59
Braby, Sue, see Caroline Arless
Brackley, 14, 19, 49, 57, 91
Brook-Popham, Lady, 70
Brown, Thomas, 18,
Buckingham, 14, 19, 92-93

Candleford, 14, 19
Candleford Green, see Fringford
Catholics, 26-28, 33-35, 106
Cavendish, Charles Compton William, see Chesham, 3rd Lord
Cheltenham Gold Cup, 62
Chesham, 3rd Lord, 54

Chesham, 5th Lord, 55
Church and Chapel, 23-35, 105-106
Coker, (Mr Coulsdon), Revd Cadwallader, 28
Collingridge, family, 33-34
Commonwealth War Graves Commission, 95-96
Corbishley, Father Samuel, 33
Cottenham, 4th Earl, 54
Cottisford, (Fordlow), 13, 15, 16, 18-19, 24, 27, 31
Cottisford enclosure and riots, 15
Cottisford House, 18, 68, 70
Cottisford Manor Farm, 19, 51
Cottisford CE School, 18, 65-67
country carriers, 86-87
cricket, 29
cycling, 88-89

Deichmann, Baron, 53
Delafield, Revd, see Thompson, Revd Charles
de Salis, Revd Henry, 65
Dewar, Arthur William, 40
Dewar-Harrison, John Francis, 40, 49, 55
Dews' Store, Fritwell, 85
Dissenters, 26, 31, 32
Drake's hounds, 53, 54

Edmund, see Timms, Edwin
education, see schools
Ellison, Revd, see Harrison, Revd Charles
Effingham, Henry Howard, 2nd Earl, 18, 33, 36, 43, 46, 51
Effingham, Henry Howard, 3rd Earl, 44, 46
Effingham, Henry Howard, 4th Earl, 44, 46
emigration, 75
End House, Juniper Hill, 16-17
evacuees, 43, 69-71

Fermor family, 33, 43
Finmere, 24, 27, 75
Finmere CE School, 64, 66, 69, 72
Finmere Station, 40, 60, 87-88
Flora, see Thompson, Flora
Florence Nightingale Lodge of the Oddfellows, 93

Friendly Societies, see Oddfellows
Fringford, (*Candleford Green*), 13, 14, 16, 19-22, 24, 27, 29, 40, 45-46, 49, 58, 75, 83, 89, 107
Fringford Forge and Post Office, 14, 19, 20
Fringford Lodge, 60, 62
Fringford Manor, 20, 70
Fringford CE School, 20, 64-66, 68-70, 72-73
Fritwell, 32, 34, 107

Godington, 24, 27, 34, 71
Gosling, Col George, 59, 60
Gosling, Capt H.M., 55
Grand National, 62
Grantham, Jimmy, 86
Grantham, William, 86
'Great Houses', 36-49, 106
Great Western Railway (GWR), 60-61,
Grenville Lodge of the Oddfellows, 92-93
Group Ministry, see Shelswell Group.

Hardwick, Old Manor House, 33
Hardwick-with-Tusmore, 24, 27, 31, 33, 92
Hardwick School, 66
Harrison, (*Revd Ellison*), Revd Charles, 18, 23, 24, 28, 65
Hethe, 24, 27, 31, 34, 35, 40, 74, 83-84, 92
Hethe CE School, 66
Hethe, St Philip's RC School, 70

Heywood-Lonsdale, Captain Arthur, 55
Heywood-Lonsdale, Col. John, 55
Hichens, Revd Anthony, 25
Hinks, Zilpha (*Zillah*), 20-21
Howard, Henry, see Effingham, Earls of
Hugh Smith, Randal, see 2nd Lord Bicester
Hugh Smith, Vivian, see 1st Lord Bicester
hunt employment, 57-60

Jennison, Revd Ronald, 25
Johnson, Charlie, 56
Johnson, Clarence, 56
Judd, Reuben and sons, 88
Juniper Hill, (*Lark Rise*), 11, 13, 14, 15-18, 22, 27, 32, 34, 74, 75, 83, 92, 105, 106
Juniper Hill allotments, 16, 80-82, 93
Juniper Hill Mob, 15, 36

Kingscote, John B., 60
Lane, Dorcas, see Whitton, Kesia,
Lark Rise, see Juniper Hill,

Laura, see Thompson, Flora
Lloyd, Revd Griff, 53
Lloyd-Mostyn, Mrs Margaret, 55

Macey, Queenie, see Massey, Eliza,
Macey, Twister, see Massey, Thomas,
Mansfield Lodge, Fringford, see Oddfellows.
Martin, Patrick, 56
Massey, Eliza, (*Macey, Queenie*), 17
Massey, Thomas, (*Macey, Twister*), 17
Matthew, see Plumb, Frederick William
Mattie Macgregor, 62
May Day, 68
McGuire, Father Alfred, 33
McMahon, Paddy, 62
Methodists, 18, 26-28, 32, 74, 105
mills, 77
Miss Pratt's, 20
Mixbury, 24, 27, 31
Mixbury CE School, 65, 66
Morgan, family, Hethe, 83, 87
Mostyn, Sir Thomas, 41
Mostyn Hounds, see Bicester Hounds
Mostyn Hunt Races, 52-53
motorcycles, 89
Mylne, Robert, 43

National Insurance, 89, 90, 92
Newton Purcell-with-Shelswell, 24, 27, 31, 52
Newton Purcell CE School, 66
Nonconformists, 27, 31-33, 35, 106
North, Lord, of Wroxton, 54

Oddfellows, Independent Order of, 89-93

Palmer, Revd William, 64,
Paxton & Holiday, 88,
Pendavis, Archdeacon Whylock, 24
Pepys, Kenelm Charles, see Cottenham, 4th Earl
Peyton, family, 51
Peyton, Sir Algernon, 4th Baronet, 41, 53
Peyton, Sir Algernon, 6th Baronet, 43, 60
Peyton, Sir Algernon, 7th Baronet, 43
Peyton, Sir Henry, 2nd Baronet, 41, 53
Peyton, Sir Henry the younger, 3rd Baronet, 41, 53
Peyton, Sir Sewster, 53
Peyton, Sir Thomas, 5th Baronet, 42-43, 53
Peyton, John, 43
Pheasey, Brian, 56

Phillimore, Claude, 48
Plumb family, Fringford, 87
Plumb, Frederick William (*Matthew*), 20, 58, 59
population, 74-76
post offices, see shops
Primitive Methodists, 32, 74

Queenie, see Massey, Eliza

railways, see travel
Ranters, see Primitive Methodists
Religious Census, 24, 26-27
Rigden, Betty, 60, 62
Rigden, family, 60
Roman Catholics, see Catholics
Roundell, Revd Henry, 33, 48, 64-65, 80
Rubio, 62

Said, Wafic, 48
schools, 64-73, 106
Selby Lowndes, family, 56
Sergeant, Revd John, 25
servants, 48-49
Shelswell airfield, 40
Shelswell Arms, 60
Shelswell Benefice, see Shelswell Group
Shelswell farms, see agriculture
Shelswell Group, 22, 24-35, 74, 106
Shelswell House, see Shelswell Park
Shelswell Playgroup, 73
Shelswell (*Skeldon*) Park, 19, 21, 36-41, 49
shops, 83-86
Slater-Harrison, (*Lady* Adelaide), Cecilia, 21, 37, 39
Slater-Harrison, Edward, (*Sir Timothy*), 19, 21, 37, 39, 40, 53, 60
Slater-Harrison, Emma Cecilia, 37, 40
Slater-Harrison, John, 38-39, 65
Smyly, Mrs, 60, 71
special trains, 60-61
Staniforth (nee Coles), Joan, 47
St Hugh's College, Oxford, 45
Stoke Lyne, 24, 27, 31, 58, 92
Stoke Lyne CE School, 66
Stratton Audley, 24, 27, 31, 51, 54-57, 58, 71, 92, 106
Stratton Audley Hall, 41, 54, 59-60
Stratton Audley Manor, 59-60
Stratton Audley Park, 55, 59-60
Stratton Audley CE School, 66

Swift's House, 36, 41-43, 49, 51, 52-53, 70

Taylor, Albert, carrier, 86
Taylor, David, 80
telephone, 85
Thompson, (*Mr Delafield)*, Revd Charles, 29
Thompson, Flora, 9, 13, 14, 15, 16, 18, 19, 21, 22, 23, 24, 28, 32, 58, 64, 74, 88, 105,106
Thornton, Martin, 56
Timms, Albert, 16, 17, 32, 43, 74, 91, 93
Timms, Edwin, (*Edmund*), 18, 23, 37, 104
Timms, Emma, 37
Timms, May, 24, 37
Timothy, Sir, see Slater-Harrison, Edward
Tomkinson, Joyce, 45
tradesmen, 82
travel, 87-89
Trotman, family, 37, 40
Tubb, Henry, 55
Tusmore Hospital, 45
Tusmore Park, 24, 33, 36, 49, 51
Tutill, George, 90-91
'Twenty-Four Square Miles', 77-78
Twister, see Massey, Thomas
Tyrwhitt-Drake, Tom, 54

Valentia, 11th Viscount, 54
von Maltzahn, Baroness Ann, 40-41

wages, 80-82
Warde, John, 51, 52
War Dead, 95-105
Westlake, Revd John, 25
Whaddon Chase Hunt, see Bicester Hunt
Whitton, Kesia (*Dorcas Lane*), 20, 21, 83-85
Wilkinson, carrier, 86
Wilkinson, William, 37
Withington, Frederick, 60, 62
women's employment, 82-83
Wyndham, Col E.H., 62

Yates, Revd Warwick (Ricky), 25

Zillah, see Hinks, Zilpha